# Roadmap to Redemption
## Revised Edition

A faith based, comprehensive workbook designed to help
survivors of exploitation overcome their past and move
forward toward their future.

## Rebecca Bender
### Survivor, Advocate & Mentor

# REVISED EDITION

Four years after writing Roadmap to Redemption, I felt a need to revise. Trauma is peculiar and time is often the key that unlocks our memory and reveals parts that we had long locked away. When I first wrote Roadmap, I hadn't had much healing. I had no trauma therapy or counseling, no EMDR or time to process. I wrote to help heal and to journal in the place that I was at in my life. As I progressed, I felt it was important to share those steps with others in hopes that they could also seek healing and purpose from their past. What I found though, is that I simply wrote it too soon. This will be a tool and example I use as we continue to mentor other survivors- jumping into things publicly before you're ready. With that being said, this is the new REVISED Roadmap to Redemption.

I've also learned a lot in the last few years of working extensively in the movement and we want to be able to use all of those insights to help others get to the next level too.

### Familial Trafficking, Survival Exploitation, etc.

One important piece I learned after using this book to mentor hundreds of trafficking survivors, is that MY experience of exploitation was through domestic pimp control. We know that is NOT the only type of human trafficking that exists. If you have been exploited by your family, a gang, survival, etc. you are NOT ALONE. This book still has incredible tips to help you heal, but in order to get the most out of it, we suggest taking the words that reference pimps or 'the life,' cross it out and write family or gang, or whatever word resonates with your situation. Don't get caught up on my experience not matching yours exactly, because these tools will still help you and traffickers tactics are the same regardless of the type of exploitation.

If you feel this book could use an addition of varying typologies, to address the nuances of other forms of exploitation, I encourage you to write your own! This field always needs more voices and experiences; so, dive in, join our online school if you desire to learn and use your passion for purpose too! We would love to come along side you and help you reach your dreams.

# PRAISE FOR ROADMAP TO REDEMPTION

"We have been waiting for a survivor leader to rise up and put an easy to understand guide together for both victims and activists. Rebecca writes just like she speaks, with confidence and familiarity. Outstanding! Roadmap to Redemption is not only a story of hope for anyone to read, but it allows victims of sexual exploitation immediate access to a mentor in the comfort of their home. This should be the go-to for any survivor looking to turn her tragedy into triumph!"

Congressman Linda Smith (1994-1999)
Founder and President Shared Hope International

"Rebecca may have written Roadmap with Christian survivors of sex trafficking in mind, but this workbook is essential for any woman who wants to work through ANY abuse or trauma in her past. If you want to dive deeper into your faith and healing, then work alongside Rebecca as she shares her truth, giving us the courage to embrace our own!"

Carissa Phelps
Author of Runaway Girl: Escaping Life on the Streets (Viking 2012)

"As an associate pastor of a fairly large church in a Seattle suburb, a leader of our Justice Council against human trafficking, and as a presenter for Community Advocates with Shared Hope International, I can say this workbook needs to be in the hands of every lay person who may find themselves in the restoration process of a survivor of human sex trafficking. Rebecca shares her story instructively with thought-provoking questions and truth blended in to gently lead a victim to the path of recovery. Her text is written as personally as she speaks, and brings the reader quickly into the setting of having a chat with a friend. As a pastor, teacher, mentor or concerned friend, you don't have to have "walked" in those shoes to be effective in standing beside a trafficked victim and help her find the way out with this tool in your hands."

Jo Lembo<br>
Associate Pastor<br>
Overcomer Covenant Church<br>
Auburn, WA

"The needs of girls who have experienced the horror of sexual exploitation are so vast. Beyond therapeutic intervention and a safe refuge for recovery, each girl needs someone she can identify with and receive advice and comfort. Rebecca is that person. The value that Rebecca 's book brings to a survivor is her experience, not just her experience of exploitation, but her experience toward healing and wholeness. Since most survivors have difficulty believing there is hope, Rebecca 's story and experience shines a light they can walk toward. I do believe this is groundbreaking both for the girl who reads it and for those who care about trafficked girls."

Mary Frances Bowley<br>
CEO/President Wellspring Living<br>
Author of The White Umbrella

"Dispelling the myths, exposing the lies and revealing the truth about being a victim of sex trafficking is what Road to Redemption is designed to do. Rebecca shares how a young woman is duped and then held captive by the very person who gave her the hope of her dreams. Once caught in the web of lies, the young woman is then forced to live a debauched lifestyle, while her boundaries, self-worth, and value are destroyed. Worse, she believes that her situation will someday change because she continues to believe in the hope her "man" once provided her! Rebecca exposes the lies of the trafficking world and presents the option of new hope and dreams to those who've suffered this cruel treatment and who need a roadmap to overcome the mental and emotional damage done to them. Roadmap to Redemption is an excellent tool for anyone who desires to learn about or be rescued from the falsehood of trafficking."

Nancy Trifilo
Author, Held Captive No More

"Rebecca has done an incredible job connecting intimately with the ready by sharing her own story and encouraging the reader to do the same. Her writing voice is relevant to the youth we work with, and they have said that they like that it "feels like she's right here with us." Thank you, Rebecca, for this extremely helpful resource for our ministry and the youth we have committed ourselves to. As one of the 16-year-olds that are going through this workbook put it, "it was exactly what I needed!"

Stephanie Holt, Executive Director
Mission 21

"This book is phenomenal! I am working through it as a survivor advocate with several others, and it has been a hard, but a positive experience. Rebecca presents truth with such love, there is no condemnation, which is something victims feel extremely easily, and it causes us to run. She understands the complexities of recovery and conveys them well. I know, myself included, her ability to express that and make light of what manipulation does to you has made us all feel a little more normal. Thank you for writing this book, it is changing lives, making those who haven't experienced this aware and compassionate, and paving the way for those who can't afford the expense of programs, centers and lots of counseling to find healing."

L. Smith, Human Trafficking Survivor

"The book was terrifying at first. You begin to understand, and can identify pimps of all kinds. It wasn't easy, but chapter 3 and on has given me such a new hope. I have been sitting down and praying over my goals. I cried as I would read them out loud because my self-esteem and hope had been ripped from me. I stopped having dreams after that and had accepted that way of life as my only obtainable life. I have never had this much confidence that I may have a future outside of trafficking and dancing. The book has encouraged me and has helped me to lay out a plan for my life after trauma."

B. Nixon, Human Trafficking Survivor

# DEDICATION

To my daughters: the greatest calling is being your mother.

I pray I never make you feel like you have to turn down a wrong path to get my time and attention. I pray that you see that the girls we are helping are someone's daughter, someone's mother, someone's sister. It is because of that that we press on toward the goal for the prize of the upward call of God in Christ Jesus.

To my husband: the greatest man I know.
Thank you for holding my hand on my journey toward redemption- I wouldn't be who I am today without you. I pray I can be as supportive and gracious as you press toward your calling.

To my sister survivors:
It is because of you that I put this on paper. Your triumphs and pitfalls have made me feel human again. May we all continue to press on toward freedom together.

# CONTENTS

# PART I - INSIDE THE MIND OF A VICTIM

# INTRODUCTION

Thank you so much for taking the time to go through this workbook with me. I am excited to get this into the hands of many people who need healing from sexual exploitation. I wish I could meet every one of you personally and pray with you throughout this journey. As a survivor myself, I have been honored to use what God has taught me along my road to redemption and pass that knowledge and wisdom, that only comes from the Holy Spirit, onto you. This work book should not be used alone but in conjunction with additional forms of trauma informed services, such as counseling, addiction, bible study, and prayer.

The healing process from sex trafficking is a lifelong journey. We don't get saved and restored and then get amnesia, unfortunately. Things will happen throughout the rest of your life that will trigger memories and emotions reminding you of the horrific trauma you have been through. This workbook is designed to help you identify when you have triggers in your life and equip you to get through them in a healthy way and hopefully dive deeper into the root of the issues so you can truly heal.

Remembering past traumas and hurts is not always easy or fun and some may ask why we have to revisit certain experiences to heal? Imagine your heart is like a beautiful garden. Over time this garden has not been cared for. Weeds have grown over some of the most amazing flowers. Fruits and vegetables that once lived there are now rotten and moldy. Going through memories is like stepping into that overgrown garden. Pulling weeds and tossing that stinky fruit is hard work and can be messy. Every time you reach a specific type of weed, think of it as an issue that has taken root in your heart. You can get rid of that issue by pulling it out at the root and filling that hole up with soil from the Holy Spirit.

Over time, the work, sweat and pricked fingers we can get from weeding, will produce a beautiful outcome. Our hearts will have abundant fruit that is ripe and sweet. The pruning of our crop will ensure a bountiful harvest that will spiritually feed ourselves and our family. Your future depends on a bountiful heart... So, let's get started!

One more thing before we get started - **You were born for greatness!** You and I are no different. The Bible tells us that God is no respecter of persons. What He did for me, He WILL do for you!

*"I am not a survivor because I escaped something horrific, I am a survivor because I allowed my pain and losses to transform me into God's instrument of greatness."*
*- Keisha Head, survivor and public speaker.*

## "You don't know the cost of the oil in my alabaster box."

### Luke 7:36-48 NLT

"One of the Pharisees asked Jesus to have dinner with him, so Jesus went to his home and sat down to eat. When a certain immoral woman from that city heard he was eating there, she brought a beautiful alabaster jar filled with expensive perfume. Then she knelt behind him at his feet, weeping. Her tears fell on his feet, and she wiped them off with her hair. Then she kept kissing his feet and putting perfume on them.

When the Pharisee who had invited him saw this, he said to himself, "If this man were a prophet, he would know what kind of woman is touching him. She's a sinner!"
Then Jesus answered his thoughts. "Simon," he said to the Pharisee, "I have something to say to you."
"Go ahead, Teacher," Simon replied.

Then Jesus told him this story: "A man loaned money to two people—500 pieces of silver to one and 50 pieces to the other. But neither of them could repay him, so he kindly forgave them both, canceling their debts. Who do you suppose loved him more after that?"
Simon answered, "I suppose the one for whom he canceled the larger debt."

"That's right," Jesus said. Then he turned to the woman and said to Simon, "Look at this woman kneeling here. When I entered your home, you didn't offer me water to wash the dust from my feet, but she has washed them with her tears and wiped them with her hair. You didn't greet me with a kiss, but from the time I first came in, she has not stopped kissing my feet. You neglected the courtesy of olive oil to anoint my head, but she has anointed my feet with rare perfume.

"I tell you, her sins—and they are many—have been forgiven, so she has shown me much love. But a person who is forgiven little shows only a little love." Then Jesus said to the woman, "Your sins are forgiven."

# CHAPTER ONE

---

## Changing the Mindset of our Culture

A lot of you reading this book may not be survivors yourself. You may be a family member or friend of someone who has experienced sexual exploitation. You may be involved in the movement as an advocate, or this is your ministry, and you want to equip yourself with tools on how to help someone who has been sex trafficked. You may just be a concerned believer who wants to hear God's story of miraculous transformation, which still takes place today. Either way, this book is for everyone! Please take the time to read the introductions to parts one and two, as they set the stage for the analogies used throughout those sections.

So, what is Human Trafficking? Usually, when most people hear that term, they tend to envision a child kidnapped, handcuffed to a bed, or stuffed in a cargo ship. When I tell people that I am a survivor of human trafficking, they usually respond, "oh like the movie Taken?" While those types of sex trafficking scenarios may take place, that is not the most common form that we see here in America.

What trafficking looks like in Thailand is different than how it looks in Cambodia, in Nigeria, New York or Boise, Idaho. If we are expecting to see human trafficking the same way in every culture, every region and every form, we will miss it every time. We, as a culture, need to start portraying a clearer picture of what human trafficking looks like in a developed, modern country like America if we want to actually identify and make a difference in our communities. Our traffickers are developed, they use deception and fraud and the internet, you can count on that.

A recent study by the Polaris Project estimates 25 different types of exploitation in America alone. That means if we are only imagining human trafficking one way, we will miss literally dozens of other types of exploitation all around us. Download Polaris' study to learn more about typologies in your area. This book will focus on domestic exploitation, and mainly pimp control. Though traffickers use similar tactics, so you will be able to identify many forms throughout.

Thirty years ago, the term Domestic Violence did not exist. Our first responders and law enforcement were not trained on how to handle "DV" situations. There was no code for the dispatch to call out over the radio. Funds were not distributed to help with shelters. Our culture saw domestic violence as a "family issue." Even in the beginning when awareness about DV began, officers were instructed to arrest the man only. After decades of awareness and training, our culture sees it differently now. Our officers arrest the primary aggressor after they get a DV call over the radio. We assist the victims in getting help and treatment. We now have the "cycle of domestic violence wheel" that our health professionals study and use. The mindset of the culture surrounding Domestic Violence has changed in the last couple decades.

Similarly, the laws on "mandated child reporting" did not exist in every state in America until 2010. How did hospital policies and procedures as well as school requirements deem this law, implement it, train on it and change protocol across America? It takes a new awareness, new facts, new research and a lot of people involved to start to understand a dangerous issue.

I believe we are on the cusp of changing the way Human Trafficking looks like in America. We are in the same early stages that domestic violence was in. As we continue to see "HT" for what it is, our first responders should receive annual training on how to differentiate between a DV and HT call. We'll hopefully have a dispatch code, professional training and prayerfully, funds distributed to assist with specialized treatment for survivors.

Did you know that the Trafficking In Persons Report (the TIP Report), which studies human trafficking worldwide annually, did not even include the United States until 2010? We were grading every country but our own. Now that advocates are starting to sound the alarm, our culture desperately needs a paradigm shift.

As survivors, we suffer from the same misconceptions. You will rarely see a victim self-identify, in the beginning, as a victim of sex trafficking. The public is waiting for a young girl to run out, clothes torn, screaming "help me I've been trafficked" as they have seen in movies and TV. But that doesn't happen. Why? Well, because we see human trafficking EXACTLY as you do. It is because all of us have this third world country view that we are no one is identifying victims and "we" aren't identifying ourselves! When I first saw the movie "Taken" I thought, *well, I'm not clawing at the carpet being pulled by a stranger out from underneath the bed. I must not be trafficked.* Therefore, I never asked for help.

"I freed a thousand slaves and could have freed one thousand
more, if only they had known they were slaves."
-Harriet Tubman

Do you see what this incorrect stigma and perception of
human trafficking creates in our society? We are looking for
something that does not exist! How can we treat and cure
cancer if we are not diagnosing it? How do we expect to treat
someone with measles if we diagnose them as having the
"flu?" Are you following me here?

So how do we identify human trafficking for what it is today,
in this developed, "civilized" country?

I love to use the analogy of a frog in boiling water: If you
were to throw a frog in a pot of boiling water, it would jump
out immediately. However, if you were to put a frog in a pot
of regular water, and put it on the stove, allowing it to heat
gradually, the frog would cook to death. That is human
trafficking. Women, young men and children, are sitting in
what appears to be regular water to them. However, it is
heating up all around them. If we do not start helping them
identify when the water is getting hot, they will "cook to
death." It is crucial to bring awareness and prevention to our
culture so that our vulnerable people can jump out before
there is any further damage.

There are several different types of Human Trafficking and in
a recent study, Polaris Project identified 25 Typologies of
Exploitation. For the sake of the persons who generally read
this book, we are going to focus on four areas:

- Familial
- Survival
- Gang Control
- Pimp Control

All of these types exist, and all of them are more or less prevalent in various parts of the country. I do encourage you to read the Typology report and research and educate yourself so you can grow in your own knowledge and understanding of the magnitude of this social injustice. It has been humbling and healing for me personally, to see the enormous amount of people who have gone before us, who are currently working tirelessly to fight for people like us. I hope that you too will feel empowered to know the amount of people who are fighting for you!

Gangs are beginning to sell people rather than drugs and guns because they do not have to replenish their supply. Rather than "jumping" in a girl, they will "sex" her in, forcing her to bring in a certain amount of money to stay in the gang. The girls also can only "work" their gang's territory. Another "benefit" gangs and drug dealers say with selling people, is that the "evidence" (the teen runaway) cannot be locked in the evidence locker, unlike drugs. This means when his trial comes up; no evidence equals no conviction and more than likely, the teen runaway is on the run again.

Familial trafficking is when we see family members force their children (or younger relative) to perform sexual acts in exchange for drugs or money. We have come across many accounts nationally where fathers make their daughters dance in the basement for his friends for money, or forces her to work in a strip club throughout high school. Fathers take their sons or daughters to truck stops. We have even seen drug addicted mothers exchange their children to every drug dealer that comes by that day for food, clothing, drugs or free rent from a landlord – anything with monetary value.

Survival trafficking is when an older adult person exploits a homeless or runaway youth for basic needs: food, shelter, even sometimes cigarettes or drugs. This adult is exploiting that person's situation in exchange for sexual favors.

Now, the type of trafficking that I am going to address in my book is primarily Pimp Control. This is because this is MY experience.

At this time, people usually ask, if people know this is going on, why aren't our law enforcement doing anything about it? Well, slowly but surely, they are! Unfortunately, though, our laws have not developed as rapidly as trafficking has. Here is a really simple way I describe it:

Prostitution is one category in most state laws.
Child Sex Abuse is another category in our legal system.

When money, or drugs, or items (food & shelter) are exchanged for sex, the "victim" is then taken out of the Child Sex Abuse Category and put in the Prostitution Category. Following me?

The problem that most states are finding is that the *Prostitution Category* does not protect victims, rather it criminalizes them. That category typically does not offer rape shield protection or proper funding for resources that a victim of violence or abuse, for example, would be entitled to. Now, don't get me wrong, there are MANY states working hard and tirelessly to make a difference. If you live in one of those states, I applaud your representative's efforts. However, it is yet to be the cultural norm, and fewer states recognize the difference in laws. Most states do not even differentiate between children and adults when it comes to prostitution. Can you imagine how many children are sitting in jail for prostitution right now? It is sad that this is how we see these victims of human trafficking. But, once again, because she wasn't dragged out from under the bed by a stranger, she must not be a victim, right? It is her fault that her father started forcing her to work in a strip club at 13 and bring men home to his basement so he could charge them.

When she solicits that first undercover cop in the club, she becomes the "criminal mastermind" that we all see her as. This is human trafficking.

So, what is PIMP CONTROL?

Have you noticed that in our society it has become common to hire a "prostitute" for a bachelor party or go to the strip club for your twenty-first birthday? What about pornography? Those are all victimless crimes, right?

WRONG! Stripping is a gateway for prostitution and often, pimps who pose as boyfriends will convince their girlfriend to start in a strip club because this expands her morals and values. It is a small, easy step to go from dancing in a club to dancing in rooms for bachelor parties, then another small step into small sexual acts, but no intercourse! Usually, the boyfriend will say something like "you don't have to do anything you're not comfortable with..." In the beginning, they will tell their "girlfriend" that she wasn't a virgin when he met her, so what's the big deal? She might as well make some money out of it. "All these other girls sleep with guys in the bar for free, at least you'll get rich doing it." It is this small, gradual expansion of boundaries that heat the water up around her.

Pimps will also go into strip clubs purposely to see if one of the girls will go out on a date with him. He is posing as an interested, potential boyfriend, but he has a plan all along. Why date a "square" girl if he could date one that is already expanded her boundaries enough on her own to get naked for strangers? Or how easy would it be to convince a girl working in a topless barista (coffee) to work topless in a strip club? See the gradual expansion?

How many pornographic images online are of girls that do NOT want their picture taken, but are posing out of the fear we don't see behind the camera?  We need to start looking behind the scenes of sexual exploitation, in all forms. That stripper that is begging to give someone a lap dance is not because she thinks they are cute or really "likes" it.  It is more than likely that her trafficker is waiting outside in the parking lot and she is short on her quota for the night. That "prostitute" is coming onto you and seeming very interested in giving exchanging a small "sexual service", not because she likes you, but because her trafficker is outside and will beat her if she doesn't meet her quota.  Oh, and guys- never ask a girl, "Do you have a pimp?" because she will NEVER admit it.  This would ruin her money- why would she do this?

### *He was my Hitler*

In November of 2013, I visited the Washington, DC Holocaust Museum. On the wall hung this profound statement that resonated within me and within this fight to eradicate modern day slavery:

"In 1932 the President of Germany heard about Hitler and the Nazi party that was rising. After receiving advice from his counsel, he offered to take Hitler under him, believing that he'd be easier to monitor and control if they had him close. Within one year, Hitler was appointed to Chancellor." So much for that idea, huh president?

So here is something for you to chew on...

If the President of Germany, a smart, older adult, intelligent man, can be manipulated and coerced into giving control of his country to a man that ruined nations and generations of people, how is it "we" can't understand how one man can use coercion to manipulate and control one vulnerable young person? You can understand and believe the history of the Nazi party, yet refuse to believe that this type of coercion, fraud, and force could convince a girl without handcuffs to

26

be sold? A girl that is already vulnerable, promiscuous, possibly abused, etc.? A girl, or any vulnerable people group!

*   Was I handcuffed to a bed? No
*   Was I kidnapped? No
*   Could I have walked away at any time? Uh.. physically walk away - sometimes, yes.
*   Was I beaten? Constantly
*   Was I coerced? I could circle 30 out of 40 on the coercion list.
*   Did I believe at first, he was my boyfriend? Yes, hence "fraud."
*   Was I brainwashed? Yes, but didn't realize that could even happen this day and age. My parents only warned me of "stranger danger."

I was as if I was the president of Germany, and he was my Hitler. I was trafficked, and yes it may not fit in a nice, neat little box to be labeled, but that doesn't mean it wasn't trafficking. Otherwise, the Feds wouldn't have raided our home. Had we talked, our trafficker would be in prison, probably serving a life sentence. But we were all too afraid... and today he walks amongst us.

The other women that were in the home I was trafficked in after we all had gotten out, one told me this:

"He beat you the most because you had a spirit that couldn't be broken."

During Hitler's reign, there were Jewish people who probably being raised as children amongst the propaganda in the education systems, simply accepted the fate that had been set before them. After growing up hearing they were *no-good*, books in schools written about the, "poisonous mushrooms," shops and stores their families owned boycotted and eventually vandalized, watching the culture pick and choose hair color and eye color and measure their noses with devices. After all of that, when the train came to pick them up, some didn't fight, some went quietly, accepting what they had been told about themselves by the culture around them. They too believed what they had been taught. A slow indoctrination.

And then there were others. Others who saw what was happening was wrong and even though they were too weak to fight by themselves, took the beatings and waited for the time to change. They had spirits that couldn't be broken. We must not only consider the indoctrination and the cultural influences, but we must also remember Fight, Flight or Freeze. When we forget the freeze, that can lead to judgement.

I want to end this chapter with the most extensive list of Human Trafficking Lingo. This will help you identify not only some of the terms used throughout my book, but maybe help you identify if a person you are working with has been trafficked and is not self-identifying yet.

One suggestion: when working with trafficked victims, NEVER use the lingo to try to get on their level or make them feel like you can identify. You may think, "I'll use the lingo, so they'll know I get it." "Maybe he or she will open up to me if I seem up on the game." The opposite is usually true. When you start acting like you have a clue what life in *the game* is like, you insult us. Not only is it insulting to pretend like you have a clue what "my life" is like, but you are reinforcing the pimp's mocking of squares. So, when you start using lingo, we hear his voice in our head making fun of you (welcome to brainwashing).

Instead, maybe start by breaking down his or her walls by saying something that she has never heard: "I am not going to sit here and pretend like I even have a clue what your life is like, but I do know that you seem to have a lot of potential and I believe you were born for greatness!"

Reinforce in them, the positive things you see, because I guarantee, they haven't heard anything about what's inside their mind or heart, in a long time! Don't get me wrong here, if you want to MIRROR them, then do it. If she calls her trafficker her boyfriend, or her man or her agent, mirror what she calls him or the other women/girls in her home because as of that moment, she believes that is what her situation is.

Before I leave you with the lingo, I wanted to share a word with you that God gave me when I first started in mentoring survivors. I was driving 4 hours one way to my first girl. I was rocking out with worship music, singing out loud. Suddenly, the presence of God fell heavy in my car. I heard the Lord ask me what would I do if one of my daughters went missing? At that moment, I felt what I can only imagine to be the actual heartache and sickness that comes from having a missing child.

I answered Him. "I'd be sick with worry. I'd call the police constantly asking about leads. I'd call every bad guy I ever knew trying to keep my ear to the streets. I probably wouldn't be able to sleep, keeping my husband up all night..."

God responded: "Exactly. These are my daughters, and there are some people out there that I will not let sleep until they're found."

So, with that- thank you for taking the time to invest in helping His daughters. It is not by chance that this epidemic is weighing heavy on your heart. He is not letting you sleep until His daughters are found. What a privilege to work for the King!

*disclaimer – I am aware that there are men, women, boys, girls and transgender that are exploited. My use of "her" or "she" is out of habit as that is who I predominantly work with. I have tried to be inclusive but you may find a slip here or there. Thank you for understanding this is not intentional, just who I serve daily in my work is women.

## HUMAN TRAFFICKING LINGO

- Bottom, or Bottom B*tch: A person appointed by the pimp/trafficker to recruit potential victims, report violation of rules, and often to help punish.
- B*tch: A term used endearingly toward one another to refer to a "working girl."
- Working: performing sexual acts for money.
- Branded: A tattoo on a victim indicating ownership by a trafficker/pimp.
- Daddy: A term a male trafficker /pimp requires his victims to call him.
- P.I. : Another term for pimp
- Family or Folks: A group of victims under the control of a trafficker/pimp. The term is an attempt to recreate the family environment.
- Gorilla (Guerrilla) Pimp: A violent trafficker/pimp
- Romeo/Finesse Pimp: A trafficker who uses fraud and deception to lure their victims in by pretending to be their boyfriend.
- Grooming: When a trafficker is dating a girl to win her trust before he tells her he is trafficker or pimp.
- Lot Lizard: Derogatory term for prostituted women and children at truck stops.
- Pimp Circle: Describes a situation where pimps circle a victim to intimidate and discipline them, using verbal and physical threats/action, i.e.,. Beating with wire coat hangers, defecating and urinating on victims

- Quota: The amount of money a victim must give to their trafficker/pimp each night. If a quota is not met, the victim may be made to work until it is, or may be beaten or otherwise disciplined.
- Seasoning: The process of breaking a victim's spirit and gaining control over her, using rapes, beatings, manipulation, and intimidation. There is a manual for pimps on how to season victims.
- Stable: A group of victims under the control of a pimp.
- Trade Up/Trade Down: The act of buying or selling a person for a pimp's stable.
- Knock: Convincing a girl to go home with a trafficker – before the "turning out" phase.
- Turn Out: To be forced into prostitution; also, a person newly involved.
- Wife-in-law or "Wifey": A term prostituted women and children are required to call the other females in the "stable."
- Sister: Another term for the other females in the stable.
- Kiddie Track or Runaway Track: Just what it sounds like it means.
- The Track/ The Blade: The area in which a girl walks to try to catch a date.
- John / Trick: A man purchasing sex from a prostituted woman or child.
- Date: The appointment set up to exchange sex for money.
- In or Out of pocket: abiding by the rules that the trafficker has set before his females.
- Reckless Eyeballing: looking at other pimps, which is considered out of pocket.
- Caught a Case: Went to jail for prostitution.

- Stack: Putting money to the side, whether a girl stacks money without permission, or the trafficker is stacking money so they can make a move
- Square: A person who is living a "normal" lifestyle
- The Game/The Life: What the entire life of human trafficking is referred to.
- Chose Up: the act of joining traffickers stable.
- Choosing Fee: A term used on girls to pay to enter the stable
- 304: "Hoe" upside down on a calculator, often used in ads or texting.

# CHAPTER TWO

---

## "I haven't been trafficked... my man loves me."

Pimps and traffickers come from all walks of life. If you are a survivor, you may be saying to yourself, "I haven't been trafficked... my situation is different." You may even think, "but he loved me; unlike some of the other stories I've heard" or "he never REALLY beat me like I hear others describe."

The truth is, if I just said exactly what you were thinking, then really your situation is NOT different. We've worked with hundreds of survivors of all types of exploitation and the hard part is that while we all have our own unique experiences, there are also a lot of similarities. It's easy to wrap our brains around force. But, understanding what fraud and coercion looks like and how it played out in our everyday lives is much more complex.

Human Trafficking usually brings an image to mind; one that we've seen in a movie or the media. Those of us who have experienced our boyfriends becoming violent and us becoming "prostitutes" can hardly relate to that image we associate as "trafficking."

However, this is the international definition of Human Trafficking:

Trafficking in persons shall mean the recruitment, transportation, transfer, harboring or receipt of persons, using the threat or use by force or other forms of coercion, of abduction, of fraud, of deception, of the abuse of power or of a position of vulnerability or the giving and receiving of payments or benefits to achieve the consent of a person having control over another person, for the purpose of exploitation. Exploitation shall include, at a minimum, the exploitation of the prostitution of others or other forms of sexual exploitation, forced labor or services, slavery or practices similar to slavery, servitude or the removal of organs;

In the beginning stages, usually, a trafficker will identify a vulnerable person who seems easy to "turn out" or "knock." He will date her (or him) for weeks or months or even just one date – each situation is different.  It is during this **grooming** phase that a bond is established.  Brainwashing and manipulation are used to then seclude his unknowing victim.  Once alone, typically, brute force or coercion and threats are then used to force the girlfriend now turned victim into prostitution.


Where did you meet your boyfriend?  If you didn't have a "man" describe where you met your trafficker, and how he *chose* you…

_____

_____

_____

_____

_____

_____

_____

_____

_____

_____

_____

_____

Usually in the moment it's hard to identify when the water is heating up around you. But this may be a time to look back and see if there was any fraud or coercion at point of recruitment?

## Identifying Pimps:

Go through carefully and circle all the ones that apply to your situation.

- Fancy car, clothes, or jewelry.
- Frequently spends nights away or out of town.
- Acts out the negative aspects of rap culture.
- No actual job that one could visit. (example: he claims to have a record label or his own magazine company, owns bill boards, restaurants, etc.)
- He has dreams of making it big and being successful. He will encourage her to become part of HIS dreams.
- Her dreams and goals for life will be put on hold for his.
- Other times, he promises to make HER dreams come true; i.e. help finishing school, or modeling, or to marry her and give her that family she always wanted.

- He pulls her into it: everything becomes "we" in her conversation. When a personal internalizes a dream, they will work harder to achieve it.
- Secludes her from family and friends by moving away.
- Attempting to fast the track the relationship (moving and talking of marriage within a short time frame should be a cause for concern.)
- Decreasing Relationships; Healthy relationships should be expanding her circle of friends.
- Carries multiple cells phones

## Identifying Victims:

- Tired during the day from working at night.
- Suddenly has expensive things: Gucci purse, diamond bracelet, name brand clothes or nails and hair done on a regular basis.
- Increasingly interested in or talks a lot about his dream, "we're going to…"
- Older boyfriend, usually one not in school.
- Morals and values have slowly expanded.
- New tattoo or "brand" of initials, his name or a saying, especially concerning money or "the life"/ "the game."
- Keeps eyes down while in public.
- Starts to become secluded, you see her less and less – even if she makes up what seems like a genuine reason for always canceling.

List how many you were able to circle:

_____

If you were trafficked in a different form, you may want to use this time to journal about grooming you experienced. Please be sure that you are ready for this step, which can be triggering. Have a trusted friend, mentor or therapist nearby to talk if needed.

My first "boyfriend" told me that he was in the entertainment industry - a music producer. I had just turned 18, and I was a single mom trying to put myself through school. I desperately wanted a family for my little girl – one I never had growing up.

The first few months were filled with gifts, dinners, and trips out of town. We spent a lot of time together. Then, I started seeing him less and less, and he said that work was demanding in larger cities: primarily in Las Vegas. That seemed normal to believe. After all, Las Vegas is the entertainment capital. We had gone to concerts before and we always went backstage. They would talk "business" even though I wasn't paying close attention, and so his cover story seemed believable.

I missed him terribly after growing so close during the first couple months. I asked him if I could go with him on business trips and he told me no.

During our grooming phase (i.e. "dating") he began expanding my boundaries. I started working at a strip club due to other influences in my life - a roommate was doing it and told me it wasn't so bad and easy money. He encouraged my involvement and took me to strip clubs when we'd make trips out of town. My aunt had been a dancer. I had become desensitized to the beginning stages of commercial sex.

The first time he took me to vacation in Vegas was a quick weekend trip. He admitted that in addition to the music group he produced and managed that there was a girl- a

37

dancer of sort, that he helped to get gigs too. He made it seem like she was making her way into the entertainment industry. He promised me they were just business partners and that he took a percentage. I believed him. My dream of a family was so close in reach – a dangling carrot of everything I had ever hoped and wanted. Young, naïve single mom me, wanted to not see any red flags.

Take some time to write about the first time you found out your boyfriend may have been into more than met the eye? How did that make you feel? Did it intrigue you that he was actually living out what others rap or sing about? He wasn't just all talk? Did it make you wonder what he was doing with other girls? Did you get jealous and wonder why you weren't enough?

_____
_____
_____
_____
_____
_____
_____
_____
_____
_____
_____
_____
_____
_____
_____
_____

During that first Vegas weekend getaway, my "man" drove me to the airport to catch my flight home. He then received a phone call from one of his girls. He was excited and praised and encouraged her proudly. He hung up and kissed me and said, "You want to upgrade your ticket to first class? She just made $3700 tonight."

I was shocked at the amount of money she made; even as a dancer I made around $300-$400 /night. This was even more! I felt special as I sat in my first-class seat all the way home that night. I had never sat first class before and was treated like someone famous by the flight staff. There were vulnerabilities in me that I didn't know I had – I wanted to feel special, to feel important to someone. I also had times in my life, that even as a normal "All-American" middle class girl, that we experienced poverty. When my mom became a single mom, we had rough times for a few years. Things turned around yes, but there were moments of vulnerabilities that I didn't know, that maybe I never saw until someone finally took the time to talk through them with me. Of course, that came later in my recovery. For that moment, I felt abundant- a false send of empowerment and abundance, but I had a taste; a taste of feeling special by him, by society when I got in that First-Class seat. I felt hope for my future for the first time in a long time.

Describe the first time your man told you about how much money you could make in the game and how it made you feel or about the first time you felt special and important and hopeful for the promises he dangled in front of you:

_____

_____

_____

_____

_____

_____

_____

_____

_____

_____

---

---

Knowing what we know about pimps, we can see a pattern if we look at my example and yours. Pimps have a process in which they manipulate and control their victims:

1 Dating
2 Grooming
3 Breaking
4 Turning Out

They lure you in with promises. They take their time to get to know your fears and dreams. This process doesn't happen overnight. Can you go back through your memories above and circle the parts where you see the first section of the process occur? First circle Dating and then circle Grooming. This dear loved one, is the epitome of fraud and coercion, it's manipulation and lies and influence that is pervasive and strong.

The Turning Out and Breaking parts are next, and they can be difficult to go through alone. Feel free to stop any time this is painful and seek your mentor, home group leader, sponsor, counselor or even a healthy friend.

* * * * *

Six months in, it happened- he invited me to move in with him. I was so excited to feel like finally the tables had turned in my life. We packed up the apartment and his brother helped us move. He drove the U-Haul with my car towed behind. I flew in a few days later with my daughter. For a long time after I believed the lie that I must not being trafficked because I got on the plane "willingly", I moved in

40

with him "willingly". This wasn't what the movies or media portrayed. Trafficked victims are only kidnapped kids overseas, right?

When I moved to Vegas to be with him, he drove me to an escort service at the end of a dead-end street. It was in a deserted strip club, no lights or signs. No one knew it was there except those who *knew* it was there. It wasn't something I found on my own, or had any understanding of how it worked or local rates, etc. He did.

He told me that going on calls for this service just like dancing in a club, that this was how it worked in Vegas, in those fancy private rooms. He said he had spent a lot of money on our move that he was using for his music business. I felt bad, I felt obligated.

Escorting sounded like prostitution. I didn't say the exact word "NO" but I showed hesitation when he told me to go in and sign up. He saw my nerves. I wanted him to love me, I wanted to please him, but I didn't quite know how to get out of this situation. He continued, "it's just like dancing in rooms, that's how dancing in those big suites works here in Vegas. It's not like you were a virgin when I met you and I'll be there… because I love you."

I still showed hesitation.  That's when he slapped me across the face. I would say it wasn't a hard slap, but that sounds like I'm excusing any abuse. But, it didn't leave a mark or make my lip bleed. I was shocked yes, but this is how adults fight right? I remember my parents yelling and throwing things against the wall after too many drinks occasionally. I remember one of my mom's boyfriends laying hands on her as an early tween. This is how adults fight… right? Maybe that's why I didn't freak out and run, I had been pre-disposed and desensitized to abuse - at least that's what my counselor has said.

In hindsight, I froze. Was any of our relationship real, did he love me at all, was our time together real? But that's when it really hit me:

I don't know where my baby was. I don't know my address by heart.

Can you remember the first time your trafficker "broke" you? Maybe yours was more or less violent than my experience. Can you identify some of the areas of vulnerabilities that normalized your response or your desire to stay even when he crossed boundaries you swore you'd never cross? Broke is not used here as dropping a glass – broke as in breaking a wild animal.

_____

_____

_____

_____

_____

_____

_____

_____

_____

_____

_____

_____

_____

That night I didn't run. Fight, Flight or Freeze. No one really knows which one they have until they are in the moment of fear and confusion and we don't always respond the same every time. I complied out of fear. I complied out of hope. I complied out of trust.

***Trafficking is not always abductions, it can also be a gradual expansion of boundaries and an increase in trust.***

The escort service was grimy and gross, but it wasn't much different than a strip club dressing room. Maybe this will be like dancing. "*My man*" drove me to a private home in Las Vegas after getting the first call. He instructed me what to say and do, how much to start with up front, etc. I give more details in my memoir, but for this workbook sake I'll keep it more about you, the reader. The first call I was taken to opened the door. The young attractive man was in his late twenties and slim with dark brown wavy hair, he reminded me of an old high school quarter back. This wasn't at all the dirty, old, stinky, fat man that the movies made me think. Maybe this won't be like the movies- maybe this is dancing – I can trust my man, he loves me. Besides in the escort service I had to sign a "will not solicit waiver" so this is just a dancing service, right?

I started lap dancing and he reached out his wallet and pulled out a little over $300. He looked confused and pulled me on top of him. I was so scared, I just froze. I didn't want to disappoint *my man*. It was over within minutes, before I could really think of what to do other than freeze. By the time it hit me: what I am doing, this isn't what I thought would happen, what do I do? it was over.

When I got in the car, he reached out his hand and asked, "how much did we make?" I told him $300 (ish) and pull it out of my purse. He took it from me and said, disappointedly, "Awe you'll do better next time. You didn't have sex for this, right?" I shook my head no. I was too embarrassed to admit that I had. Next time? I just stared out the window and let the tears fall. I didn't want him to see me crying. This isn't quite the happy future I imagined when packing my apartment.

Can you remember the first time you turned a trick It wasn't quite what you had imagined was it?

_____

_____

_____

_____

_____

_____

I was driving to several calls that night and I was able to push my fear down until it was suffocated by adrenaline. For the first weeks, he drove me. I thought it was because he wanted to make sure I was safe and help me maneuver the big city and back roads that I had to learn. Looking back, I realized he wanted the money after each call, and he wanted to make sure I didn't spend any of it on something that didn't meet his approval.

I came to that realization the hard way only short while in in Vegas. He had me catch a cab for my last call because he had an "entertainment client" in town. I went on a two-girl call with a red head who had been there a long time. She invited me to breakfast after the call and offered to drive me home. I was flattered and felt like a new girl at school being asked to sit at the cool kid's table. She was pretty and fun and experienced, and I didn't have any friends – I wasn't really allowed to be around anyone other than him, his brother, my daughter and the buyers. I was being socially ostracized and didn't even know it.

I walked in the house after breakfast around 7 am. I was greeted with a slap across my face. He began to berate me, put me down, criticize my stupidity and made me feel ashamed. Why was he treating me this way? He said that she didn't want to be my friend, that she was going to try to convince me to join her "family." I thought he was wrong; she and I clicked. But, after all, he did know best. He had been there longer than I had. I desperately didn't want to ruin my relationship and hope to get out of this wealthy and normal. I'd do what he said so that we could get back to being happy.

Explain the first time your man got upset with you. Hitting is not the only way that abuse occurs. Describe what happened and how it made you feel:

_____
_____
_____
_____
_____
_____
_____
_____
_____
_____
_____

Can you go back through your last two memories now and identify where the last two parts of the manipulation process took place:

3. Breaking
4. Turning Out

This entire process pimps use to make us believe our situation is different, is part of their brainwashing, manipulation and control tactics.

Your situation may not have been with a pimp, or you may not identify as being exploited through The Life/The Game. Can you cross out the name "my man" and replace it with what you knew your trafficker as? Can you go back and think of the times you were groomed and turned out? When working with those who have experienced familial trafficking, the same grooming, expanding of boundaries, since of obligation, lack of choice, turning out, is all similar. There is nothing new under the sun and the same evil spirit that exploits the vulnerable can be identified. For more on identifying your vulnerabilities, grab our Elevate Toolkit or join us at the Elevate Academy.

Here are a few reminders from the word of God that He is concerned about what concerns you:

The Lord hears his people when they call to him for help. He rescues them from all their troubles. The Lord is close to the brokenhearted; he rescues those whose spirits are crushed. Psalm 34:17-18 NLT

You keep track of all my sorrows. You have collected all my tears in your bottle. You have recorded each one in your book. Psalm 56:8 NLT

Are not five sparrows sold for two pennies? Not one of them is forgotten by God. Indeed, the very hairs of your head are all numbered. Don't be afraid; you are worth more than many sparrows. Luke 12:6-7; Matthew 10:29-31 NLT

# CHAPTER THREE

---

## Power of Coercion: 40 reasons she won't leave

 

The human trafficking definition states that a person will use force, fraud or coercion.  But, what is coercion? What is an actual real-life example of coercion?  Can you list one?

_____

_____

Don't worry; I couldn't either!  Actually, after nearly six years of trafficking, I had been through three pimps, two brandings (tattoos), several attempted escapes and two rehab facilities and more!  I still had no clue what coercion even was. Understanding the complexities of coercion played out in everyday life was harder than people realize. It takes time and can be really hard to work through these memories.

I came home to visit my family one holiday and had a black eye that I had been trying desperately to cover up.  My aunt worked for a domestic violence shelter at that time.  She handed me a paper before I left on my flight back home that was titled: "Why She Won't Leave."

The following information came from various batterer's intervention projects, therapy groups used to rehabilitate domestic violence offenders, and domestic violence agencies that work with the survivors of abuse. The tactics listed below are from the mouths of abusers themselves. I have adapted it to fit traffickers and pimps specifically and added survivor's thoughts.

The list is mind blowing to read. Our situation is not different if everyone is doing and thinking the same thing. Reading the list was like a splash of cold water in my face, and even though it's hard, I hope it will be one for you too because it's helpful to start to identify coercion and fraud. It puts the blame back on the perpetrator, not on us! This chapter is usually the hardest for most survivors. It can make feel stupid and ashamed to have been deceived. Please don't even entertain that lie. This list is to show you that IT WAS NOT YOU! You did nothing wrong.

I'd like you to go through this list and circle every tactic that you KNOW took place or you can identify with. Remember these are actual statements from abusers themselves:

## I WOULD ISOLATE HER, BREAKING HER TIES WITH ANY SUPPORT SHE HAD:

- I convinced her/him family and friends that I was the good one.
(Survivor: "He met my parents, and they liked him." "He helped my family during hard times.")
- I took all of the money so that she/he depended on me for everything.
(Survivor: "At first, I felt I was a contributor to the home, but then I questioned why he had to control

EVERYTHING. He insisted that he take me to the grocery store. He paid the power bills; he mocked me if I didn't eat what he ate.")

- I would start a fight before she/he visited with friends and family so that eventually, she/he just stopped visiting.

(Survivor: "I felt too guilty about leaving after an argument. I was also too embarrassed for my family to see my bruises.")

- I moved her/him way out in the country or to another city. When I left, I took her car battery with me.

(Survivor: "At first, I felt excited to be on a new adventure, a new town. After a while, I felt I had no one to turn to – nowhere to go.")

- I convinced the people around her/him that she/he was crazy, imagined things, and needed counseling. I could prove it by pointing out her/his erratic behavior. That way, she/he had nowhere to go if she/he tried to leave.

(Survivor: "I remember thinking, 'Am I crazy?' I couldn't follow the conversation because he kept talking in circles.")

- I convinced everyone around her/him that she was incapable of caring for the children because of her stupidity, mental illness, and laziness.

(Survivor: "He convinced me that I would lose my child if anyone knew what was going on in our house.")

- I ripped the phone cord out of the wall during a fight when she/he tried to call for help or broke her/his cell phone.

(Survivor: "He even controlled who I called on my cell. I felt sick to my stomach as he read my text messages wondering if the smallest thing would set him off.")

- I had her/him back me up on illegal things so that I could hold it over her/his head if she tried to leave.

(Survivor: "He would tell me that he'd turn me in if I tried to leave.")

## I'D MAKE HER DOUBT HER SANITY AND CAPABILITIES:

- I'd convince her/him that she/he was crazy by playing mind games with her. I'd hide her things, and tell her how incompetent she/he was so that she'd/he'd believe me when I told her/him that she/he needed me. (known as: gas lighting)

(Survivor: "I felt that something was WRONG with me. I questioned my sanity.")

- I kept her/him up for the night, so she/he was easier to control the next day.

(Survivor: "I remember feeling 'crazy.' He'd fight with me when I returned from work. I'd kept wanting to just go to sleep.")

- I turned the kids against her/him by making her/him the bad parent and tricking the children. I would make her discipline the children by threatening to hit them harder if she/he didn't and then I'd threaten to report child abuse if she/he left me.

(Survivor: "I thought, 'If I hit them, it'll hurt less; if I let him do it, it will hurt more.'" "I feared the day when my little one got old enough to talk back to him.")

- I made her feel guilty about wanting to break up our family, that she was a bad mother and wife if she wanted to leave every time things got difficult.

(Survivor: "He'd say that people who love each other stick it out through rough times – that we could get through this, and I'd think to myself, 'he'll change.'")

- I told her how fat and ugly she was all the time, and how badly she did things around the house. I told her how embarrassed I was of her.

50

(Survivor: "I wanted him to adore me, so I tried hard to do things to get his approval." "He didn't let me come home until I lost weight.")

- I told her that no one else would want my sloppy seconds, that she was used goods; that no one would want to marry a whore.

(Survivor: "No one else will understand. Who wants to marry a prostitute?")

- I'd rape her.

(Survivor: "I kept wondering why he was doing this to me. I left for a while but then he came to find me. No one knew that I'd been raped.")

## I MADE HER AFRAID OF LEAVING ME:

- I told her that women's shelters were for women who needed it, not for women who wanted to give up on their family, not for whores and prostitutes. Only weak women live in those places.

(Survivor: "I believed him. I believed that the shelter staff would not take me in; thinking that it was my choice. I didn't want to appear weak.")

- I made sure she knew that she wouldn't get a dime from me if she left and that she'd be poor and homeless. I ruined her credit by putting things in her name and not paying them.

(Survivor: "He told me, 'you leave with what you came with.' Even though I had lots of things and made lots of money, I couldn't take any of it with me.")

- I followed her without her knowing so that I could make her believe I had people watching her.

(Survivor: "I thought there were cameras in my car. I thought I was crazy as I searched for the camera." "He knew all my actions – what I'd done the day before. He said he'd dreamt it."

- I threatened suicide.

(Survivor: "I felt like he needed me.")

- I told her I would kill her.

(Survivor: "I believed him.")

- I threatened to hurt people she loved.

(Survivor: "I knew he was capable of this. I would do anything to protect them. The abuse was a 'small price to pay' to keep them safe.")

- I would lock up all of her things, including the social security cards, birth certificates, and pictures. I'd take things that were important to her so she'd come back or reach out.

(Survivor: "I thought, 'How am I going to start again? I feel hopeless.'")

- I broke things and told her that it was her fault for upsetting me.

(Survivor: "I knew better than to do what made him mad. I should get my mind right.")

- I reminded her of the last time she left me, that it only made things worse.

(Survivor: "I thought, 'he's right; it did get worse last time I tried to leave.'")

- I told her that I'd never let her go, no matter what it took.

(Survivor: "I thought, 'He loves me that much that nothing can separate our love.'")

- I convinced her that I'd find her wherever she went.

(Survivor: "He had.")

- I laughed and told her about men that had violently hurt (or murdered) their ho's when they tried to leave.

(Survivor: "He threatened to take me to his friend's house to have them burn me or douse me with gasoline. I knew they had done it to others, so I was afraid.")

- I always kept one of the kids with me so I knew that she'd always come back.

(Survivor: "How could I leave my step son to take all of my pimp's anger? The children couldn't handle it.")

## I CONVINCED HER THAT I DESERVED ANOTHER CHANCE:

- I convinced her that I was sorry for what I'd done.
(Survivor: "He said he knew he had problems and he wanted to change")
- I cried to her.
 (Survivor: "I believed him.")
- I promised to change my ways.
(Survivor: "It got better for a while.")
- I promised to go to drug and alcohol treatment.
(Survivor: "He looked up class times online and they all conflicted with his schedule. Well, he tried.")
- I promised to go to counseling.
(Survivor: "But how could a square doctor understand our lifestyle? I didn't want him to subject himself to that kind of judgment, so I insisted he didn't.")
- I blamed the abuse on stress.
(Survivor: "I thought, 'we are going through a lot right now. It will get better soon.")
- I romanced her with flowers, took her shopping, talking about all the good times, and telling her how much she meant to me.
(Survivor: "I thought, 'This is how things are supposed to be. . . if only *I'd* start acting right.")
- I even arranged for us to take a romantic trip together to get back on track.
(Survivor: "We went to Mexico on a week's vacation. He took me and the kids to Disneyland.")
- I made her think she needed to stick with me because of all I gave up to be with her.
(Survivor: "I reminded myself: '*people in love stick it out through rough times. You don't just give up.*'")

- I made her feel sorry for me, and that her love could change me.

(Survivor: "I believed our love was that strong.")

- If she didn't have children, I'd introduce her to mine and tell her I wanted a family with ONLY her because she was special.

(Survivor: "I believed, 'our situation is different. I am different than other girls.'")

- I'd give her a night off and rent movies and spend quality time to convince her that I cared.

(Survivor: "I thought, 'This is how life will be when we finally have enough money.'")

---

How'd you do?  I wish I were sitting with you during this section beloved.  I'd hold your hands and let you cry.  This is the moment that usually the scales begin to lift from our eyes. Even years after recovery from my trauma, I still had a hard time believing that not one inkling of my pimp cared about me.  I thought somewhere in his heart he cared a little.  Your pimp cared about you as much as you cared about your first trick; remember him?  Never forgotten, but never loved.

I'm not sure if this part will ever get easier. Even as I write this 2nd edition, ten years after escaping, it's hard to think that not a moment of his time or energy actually cared.  You know what helped me really understand that? I was reunited with a woman I was trafficked with. She told me about complaints he made or comments he would say. She didn't say it to hurt me, she said it as if I had already known. It stung and reminded me that I was only a money maker for him.

Those of you who have experienced familial trafficking, it is hard to consider that your family, the people who should love and protect you are the very people that hurt you. This is so incredibly hard and probably the root of boundary and trust issues that can continue to follow us. I encourage you to jump onto Elevate Connect to surround yourself with a community of survivors who have been through familial trafficking. Together we CAN lean on one another. Because family should NEVER hurt you.

Take some time with Jesus right now. Holy Spirit, show my survivor sister or brother, that they are special to someone and his name is Jesus. Hold them like the precious son and daughter that they are God, and gently remove the scales slowly from their eyes. In Jesus name.

You ready for a word from God? I just love when God gives us scriptures to heal our wounds like a band aid on a scrape or in my case, and maybe yours too, stitches for my deep stabbings.

## Isaiah 43: 1-7
1 But now, O Israel, the LORD who created you says: "Do not be afraid, for I have ransomed you. I have called you by name; you are mine. 2 When you go through deep waters and great trouble, I will be with you. When you go through rivers of difficulty, you will not drown! When you walk through the fire of oppression, you will not be burned up; the flames will not consume you. 3 For I am the LORD, your God, the Holy One of Israel, your Savior. I gave Egypt, Ethiopia, and Seba as a ransom for your freedom. 4 Others died that you might live. I traded their lives for yours because you are precious to me. You are honored, and I love you. 5 "Do not be afraid, for I am with you. I will gather you and your children from east and west 6 and from north and south. I will bring my sons and daughters back to Israel from the distant corners of the earth. 7 All who claim me as their God will come, for I have made them for my glory. It was I who created them."

Do you know anyone that has died or been wounded by exploitation? Anyone who has lost their children or still to this day feels hopeless about their future? Go back through the above Bible passage and cross out the names: Egypt, Ethiopia and Seba in verse 3 and write their names in that place. Reread the scripture again.

We occasionally have people join us who have been through SRA or whose abuser has used scripture over them to control and threaten. Please remember that the word of God can be a lamp unto our feet and a light unto our path. Evil will try to distort the word of God, but don't let evil win here. Ask the Holy Spirit what parts of the scripture he wants you to focus on and don't fall into the trap of thinking of this group as evil. That is exactly what the enemy wants is for you to turn away and close your ears. This is a great time to reach out to your mentor, your counselor your pastor or coach and learn more about inner healing work around this scripture. Triggers are real and normal, but we are here to help not hurt you.

***You were born for greatness beloved!*** God chose you from all corners of the earth to come out victorious. He has an amazing plan for your life.

"No eye has seen, no ear has heard, and no mind has imagined what God has prepared for those who love him." - 1 Corinthians 2:9 NLT

"For I know the plans I have for you," declares the LORD, "plans to prosper you and not to harm you, plans to give you hope and a future. - Jeremiah 29: 11 NIV

Do you know someone else who died that you might live? Jesus. This may be hard for those of you who are not into the whole "faith" thing yet to believe or understand, but God sent his only son to die on the cross for you. He fulfilled every Old Testament covenant once and for all, so that we

56

could have full access to God without a priest, so that we wouldn't have to give sacrifices to forgive sins, we can do directly to Him – to Abba Father. All God and Jesus truly want is a relationship with you. Not a relationship like your man or your parents gave, one you've never experienced before.

I "challenge" you in a sense, to give God the same amount of time that you have given a life of trafficking, or that trafficking took from you. If your trafficker took six years of your life, try to give God six years of your life before you give up on the idea of a healthy, happy future. Wait, watch and follow Him and see what He can do. He loves you deeply. Ask Jesus into your heart to begin this process, "Jesus, I believe you are the son of God who died on the cross for my sins and rose three days later. Come into my heart and renew my mind and spirit. In Jesus name, Amen."

I can actually remember being frustrated with my healing one year into trying to live normal. After one frustrating day of being self-aware of all my very real flaw and negative character habits I had developed, the Lord said something very powerful:

### *"If you give me the same amount of time that you gave your pimp, I promise, I will never be outdone."*

Other Factors:
There are various reasons we are "chosen" by a pimp to be turned out. Our home life growing up, our hope for a future we never had or one we wanted desperately for our kids are just a few examples. Maybe it's our self-worth and value system that made it easy for a pimp to lure us into his clutches. Let's try to find some roots in your life that may have caused you to be easily deceived. There is no shame in being deceived. The Bible says our hearts are deceitfully

wicked.  God is not upset with you nor does He think any less of you.

He is nothing like your pimp, nor is He anything like your father.  Jesus is not the police holding a baton over you ready to get you in trouble either.

You are His daughter.  I have a one-year-old daughter right now.  When she poops on the floor while I run to get a diaper after the bath, or hits her older sister, I don't discipline her.  The opposite is true- I usually laugh and think "she is so stinking precious."  God does the same with you.  When you behave in a way that may not seem "correct," He just smiles and thinks you're precious.  Don't get me wrong... God DOES discipline those He loves, but I believe that will come in time.  For now, in the beginning, while you are an infant spiritually, a newborn in Christ, He just wants to love you like a mother would love a baby.  The discipline and correction and guidance comes as we grow in Him.

So, let's talk briefly about what made you so vulnerable to a pimp.  What was your childhood like?  Divorced or married parents?  Siblings?  Was there abuse in your home?  Our childhood could be an ENTIRE work book.  We don't want to focus on that too much because my hope is that you are receiving help with those issues separately.

I can remember as a child never feeling important or loved.  I won't go into too much detail, but like most going through this workbook, I did experience some violence in my home as a child, but I was never sexually molested, never was put in foster care or had CPS called.

My mom left my alcoholic father only to move in with her abusive boyfriend.  She was too busy picking up her life to notice mine and my dad was too busy drinking to notice me either.  I felt alone, unloved and unimportant.  It didn't take much for my boyfriend turned pimp to lure me out with feelings of love, importance, and family.  Can you ask the Holy Spirit to identify some feelings like the ones I listed that made it easy for your pimp?

_____

_____

_____

_____

_____

_____

_____

_____

_____

_____

_____

_____

_____

_____

_____

_____

_____

_____

_____

_____

_____

_____

_____

_____

_____

_____

_____

_____

_____

_____

_____

_____

_____

Ezekiel 16:4-19 NLT

"On the day you were born, no one cared about you. Your umbilical cord was not cut, and you were never washed, rubbed with salt, and wrapped in cloth.  No one had the slightest interest in you; no one pitied you or cared for you. On the day you were born, you were unwanted, dumped in a field and left to die.

"But I came by and saw you there, helplessly kicking about in your blood. As you lay there, I said, 'Live!'  And I helped you to thrive like a plant in the field. You grew up and became a beautiful jewel. Your breasts became full, and your body hair grew, but you were still naked.  And when I passed by again, I saw that you were old enough for love. So I wrapped my cloak around you to cover your nakedness and declared my marriage vows. I made a covenant with you, says the Sovereign LORD, and you became mine.

"Then I bathed you and washed off your blood, and I rubbed fragrant oils into your skin.  I gave you expensive clothing of fine linen and silk, beautifully embroidered, and sandals made of fine goatskin leather.  I gave you lovely jewelry, bracelets, beautiful necklaces, a ring for your nose, earrings for your ears, and a lovely crown for your head.  And so you were adorned with gold and silver. Your clothes were made of fine linen and were beautifully embroidered. You ate the finest foods—choice flour, honey, and olive oil—and became more beautiful than ever. You looked like a queen, and so you were! Your fame soon spread throughout the world because of your beauty. I dressed you in my splendor and perfected your beauty, says the Sovereign LORD.

"But you thought your fame and beauty were your own. So, you gave yourself as a prostitute to every man who came along. Your beauty was theirs for the asking. You used the lovely things I gave you to make shrines for idols, where you played the prostitute. Unbelievable! How could such a thing ever happen? You took the very jewels and gold and silver ornaments I had given you and made statues of men and worshiped them. This is adultery against me! You used the beautifully embroidered clothes I gave you to dress your idols. Then you used my special oil and my incense to worship them. Imagine it! You set before them as a sacrifice the choice flour, olive oil, and honey I had given you, says the Sovereign LORD."

That scripture is crazy, huh? It brings both good and bad feelings to the surface for me. It makes me feel bad for the things I did with my life. I have asked God to forgive me for the things I did with the life He gave me.

It also makes me feel like God understands a little bit. The Bible was written thousands of years ago. Prostituted persons were written about from the beginning. There are WAY more accounts of prostitution in the bible than I ever remember my Sunday School teacher talking about.

Rahab was one of the most influential prostituted women and brothel owners in her time- not only did she help the army of God and the angels of death spared her and her family, but she ended up being in the lineage of Jesus! You see, God loves girls just like us.

The passage from Ezekiel helps me feel closer to the Lord. While He never approved of my choices, He has always understood and He is waiting for my reconciliation to Him. Go back and underline parts of the above passage that really stand out to you. Then, write about how this scripture changes the way you may have thought about God…

_____
_____
_____
_____
_____
_____
_____
_____
_____
_____
_____
_____
_____
_____
_____
_____
_____

One night in my drug induced stooper, my pimp and I got in a fight. I had been using drugs a lot. Looking back, I realized it was to mask the feelings of shame and embarrassment of what my life had become. All I knew was that it made me feel good for the first time in a long time.

My pimp got mad at me for continuing to pay the dope man before him. He hit me, and in that instance, I had enough drug enhanced courage to fight back. It was like a scene out of Ike and Tina Turner's What's Love Got To Do With It.

He left angry, and I sat on the kitchen floor bloody, bawling uncontrollably. I was crying out loud "Why won't he love me? What more could I do for him?"

As I started getting to know Jesus, I was in prayer one morning when he brought that night to mind. The feelings of heartbreak came to the surface. "That's how I felt about you…" Jesus whispered.

Do you know that Jesus was broken, bloody and battered on the cross for you? Every time he beckoned us and we turned away, can you picture him wondering why you wouldn't love him? Thinking of Jesus as a man, in the same vulnerable situation that we have been, makes Him a little more human, doesn't it? I know Jesus loves you so much that He gave His life you.

_____

_____

_____

_____

You did great today! We got a lot of cold water thrown in our face, and you took it gracefully. Don't give up on the weeding process now! Over the next couple days, before we move forward, I strongly encourage you to wake up thirty minutes earlier than normal. Turn on some worship music and get down on your knees. Start singing along with the music and ask the presence of God to fall in your room. A few minutes at the feet of Jesus will do more than hours of counseling. You're not the same after you physically experience the love of Christ, you can't help but come out changed after being in the presence of the King.

# CHAPTER FOUR

---

## Breaking the Myths: Changing the mindset of a culture

We have talked a lot about the definition of trafficking. Before you started this work book, how would you have described trafficking? Close your eyes and imagine a trafficked girl. What does she look like? What is she doing?

_____

_____

_____

_____

_____

Now that you have been shown ways a pimp manipulates, controls, uses coercion and violence, has your image of trafficking changed? _____

_____

_____

_____

So, what happens when a girl has gone from pimp to pimp to pimp? Is it her choice? We're going to spend this chapter doing exactly what the title says: Breaking the myths. Have you heard some of these terms when you were in the game or the life?

*     Choose Up
*     Choosing Fee
*     Who you gonna choose?
*     Your *ho* chose me

The use of the word "choose" has had a subtle, yet impactful way on how we as victims have agreed with the lie that our situation is our choice.

The power of human trafficking is so strong that even in situations where we may have had the opportunity to "run," we stayed. We found a lesser of two evils and went with another P.I. Or maybe after years of having our dream dangled in front of us with no end in sight, we found it easy to believe that a different man could help us finally succeed. You see, there is something special about girls like us.

WE WERE CHOSEN… BY GOD!
We do have success and purpose birthed in our hearts and spirits, but it is a God given desire that has been tainted by the things of this world.

At one point in my life I left my pimp after a couple years of extreme drug use. I believe he was happy to see me go since he didn't fight to keep me. I was a troubled girl who desperately wanted all his love and attention. I used a lot of drugs to medicate my heart and mind and caused chaos to his other girls with severe competition and fighting. Can you think of some things you did to self-medicate? If not drugs and alcohol, how about cutting or eating to numb your pain? What did your self-sabotage, (or coping mechanism), do to you and your pimp/traffickers relationship?

_____

_____

_____

_____

I spent eighteen months in a Christian rehabilitation home:
Victory Outreach. God used that as an instrument for my
salvation. After this spiritual boot camp, I got a real job at a
well-known cell phone store in the mall. I remember walking
by Starbucks on my way to work one day, thinking about the
cup of coffee that I could not afford. My daughter and I
would ride the public bus in the morning from my bunk bed
equipped, one-bed room apartment, downtown to her
daycare. Then, I'd get back on the bus and ride it uptown to
work. Months went by like this, and I became depressed.
The bills never stopped, and decorating from yard sale finds
got discouraging. Was I ever going to catch a break? Was
this the life that God promised me?

The addiction to money had never surfaced during my
recovery. I dealt solely with my drug addiction and
deliverance, and I was incredibly thankful for my newfound
salvation. I knew God used this facility significantly to
establish a deep relationship with Jesus. But, I had yet to
identify as a trafficked victim. I thought my problem was
drugs and that I "chose a bad boyfriend" who abused me- he
happened to be a pimp, and I chose a life of prostitution. See
that word "chose" in my thought process? It was a lie and
brainwash that I had become indoctrinated with.

So here I was walking by Starbucks daydreaming about that
cup of coffee, allowing the devil to use my mind as a
playground and become ungrateful for the blessings I had
received.

I had no treatment to pull from for issues other than drugs.

The need to feel important never surfaced during my recovery...
The trauma of being sexually exploited was never addressed.
I was never taught how to budget on a real salary...

I'd lie in bed and entertain the thoughts of working in Vegas one last time. With no drug habit and no pimp, could I possibly make enough to buy a home? Then I wouldn't mind living off a normal income, right? This is also key as to why specialized treatment for sex trafficking survivors is needed not just rehab or a DV shelter. Hey, if that's the only thing available to get away, praise God, but victims need MORE based on the brainwashing thought patterns that have been established.

You see where this is going? It was a set up by Satan himself. Soon enough, a charming, attractive man walked into my store. He laid five hundred dollars cash down on my counter and asked to buy the Motorola Razor. I knew he was a pimp.

I jumped in the car with him that week and left for Vegas shortly after. Most girls at this point can identify with a time in their life when they either did choose another pimp or at least considered it. Entertaining those thoughts can give you the illusion that it is our choice.

Have you ever had a similar experience with another pimp? Has there been times in your life when you felt that your situation was your "choice?" Describe the brainwash and self-blame that you want to shake today:

_____

_____

_____

_____

_____

_____

_____

_____

_____

_____

_____

_____

_____

_____

_____

_____

_____

_____

_____

_____

_____

_____

_____

_____

_____

_____

It is hard sometimes to internalize the truth that living a life of human trafficking can brainwash a person to believe that this is the only option available to them. It can be difficult to get out of the madness in our head sometimes. The Bible gives us some tips on how to fight those battles. We'll address those in Chapter 6: Spiritual Warfare.

Please get out your bible and read Psalms 40 (or it is below if you need it). Don't worry; there are only 16 verses. Write down the one in the space provided, that stands out the most to you.

1. I waited patiently for the Lord to help me, and he turned to me and heard my cry.

2. He lifted me out of the pit of despair, out of the mud and the mire. He set my feet on solid ground and steadied me as I walked along.

3. He has given me a new song to sing, a hymn of praise to our God. Many will see what he has done and be amazed. They will put their trust in the Lord.

4. Oh, the joys of those who trust the Lord, who have no confidence in the proud or in those who worship idols.

5. O Lord my God, you have performed many wonders for us. Your plans for us are too numerous to list. You have no equal. If I tried to recite all your wonderful deeds, I would never come to the end of them.

6. You take no delight in sacrifices or offerings. Now that you have made me listen, I finally understand - you don't require burnt offerings or sin offerings.

7. Then I said, "Look, I have come. As is written about me in the Scriptures: 8 I take joy in doing your will, my God, for your instructions are written on my heart."

9. I have told all your people about your justice. I have not been afraid to speak out, as you, O Lord, well know.

10. I have not kept the good news of your justice hidden in my heart; I have talked about your faithfulness and saving power. I have told everyone in the great assembly of your unfailing love and faithfulness.

11. Lord, don't hold back your tender mercies from me. Let your unfailing love and faithfulness always protect me.

12. For troubles surround me—too many to count! My sins pile up so high I can't see my way out. They outnumber the hairs on my head. I have lost all courage.

13. Please, Lord, rescue me! Come quickly, Lord, and help me.

14. May those who try to destroy me humiliated and put to shame. May those who take delight in my trouble turned back in disgrace.

15. Let them be horrified by their shame, for they said, "Aha! We've got him now!"

16. But may all who search for you filled with joy and gladness in you. May those who love your salvation repeatedly shout, "The Lord is great!"
17. As for me, since I am poor and needy, let the Lord keep me in his thoughts. You are my helper and my savior. O my God, do not delay.

_____
_____
_____
_____
_____
_____
_____
_____
_____
_____

Why do you think this specific scripture stands out?  Is there a memory or feeling that surfaces in your heart when you read it? _____
_____
_____
_____

I can tell you, that so many in this chapter stand out for me, it's hard to pick just one!  That my sins pile up so high that I cannot see my way out; that they are more than the hairs on my head.  That he heard my cry and took me out of the muck and the mire, that many would see and be amazed and because of that trust the Lord... That he steadied me as I walked along...

That word "steadied" in Greek is **kuwn** and means: to fix, to make ready, to prepare, provide, provide for, furnish

Oh, beloved sister, He will fix you along this path, He will make you ready, He will prepare you for your future, He will provide for you, and He will furnish your new life to come! Believe that because His word NEVER lies. Though many may have ran some game on you, God NEVER does!

Another myth I want to break is that you will be excited and happy to be "rescued" and ready for the healing process. The opposite is usually truer.

At first, it seems as if the people surrounding you are taking away the future that you had attached yourself to. You are angry at them for ruining your dream. If you had just had a little more time, it would have all worked out. As soon as that car was bought, things would start coming together. As soon as you got your place furnished, things would start falling into place. Wrong. Wrong. Wrong.

You were created to be in relationship with God. He is the missing piece in your life. No other tangible thing will fit in His place. It is like trying to force a round peg into a square hole or trying to force the piece of that jig saw puzzle into the place it just doesn't belong. Your life will only come together perfectly when all the pieces fit, and if you are not putting Jesus in His rightful place, you will be continually chasing something else to fill that hole.

Could you walk barefoot in the woods for years without developing callused feet? Nor can you live in the game without callused hearts. Addressing all the issues that stem from sex trafficking is crucial to your future.

Look at this boundary box example:

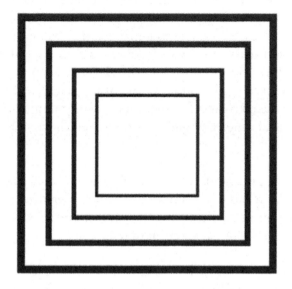

When you first were a child, your morals and values were small. You had the pleasure of innocence. Then, with the first lie you told your parents, or the first drink you had a party, your boundary box expanded. You may have been raised in a home with violence or drug use. That only means your boundary box started out larger than others.

With each small step away from innocence, your boundaries expanded. Mine went from watching domestic violence in my home to drinking and smoking at parties, to using drugs in high school, to sleeping with boys for attention, to dancing in a strip club, to selling my body, to being accepting of abuse.

Take some time to label the boxes of your life in the diagram provided.


Shrinking our morals and values back down to a normal size is not comfortable.
Have you ever tried to lose weight?  At first, you cut down on your portion sizes.  You will also probably set up a plan to not eat refined flours or sugars.  You'll try to keep your caloric count to a minimum.  None of this is easy.  If you have ever dieted, you can remember cravings, hunger pangs, possibly head aches and guilt when you fell short and cheated.

Shrinking your boundary box down to a "normal" size will have similar feelings.  It is not easy, and it is painful but remember, just like dieting gets you a beautiful new healthy body, the results are a beautiful new life.

Therefore, if anyone is in Christ, he is a new creation; old things have passed away; behold, all things have become new.
- 2 Corinthians 5:17 NKJV

Below are some "boundary pangs" we'll call them, like "hunger pangs," that can surface while God transforms our minds into healthy and fit members of our body.
Hardened:  We can be hard, mean and rough. We have had to compartmentalize emotions to keep ourselves sane; we have had to turn off certain emotions to get by. It's hard to turn off only one emotion; when you turn off one, you turn off them all. Our souls are like rock hard clay that will take a lot of watering to soften.  Holy Spirit wants to water your soul with encouragement, praise, and structure to get that heart of stone softened and molded into a heart of flesh. It is not easy at first to let our emotions mingle, to let our guards down and open up to people. Try to be vulnerable and transparent with those around you. Don't put up a front or a wall, out of fear.

Running Drag: You may call this something different, but it is when you have to get out of a sticky situation in the game, or you make up a story to get more money from a trick. This "skill" has become your second nature, like snake skin needing to be shed. This is a learned behavior and needs to be reversed. Work on watching what you say to others and even what you say to yourself and God. God calls this lying, and it is deadly to our future. Start small by actually watching how you tell a story. Is there any ounce of embellishment or exaggeration?

Denial is a form of coping: It is embarrassing to admit that you have been deceived, that you have believed the lies for so long. More often than not, it takes TIME to convince us that we have even been trafficked. Coming out of denial can be painful, shameful and embarrassing. Let yourself feel these shrinking pains by hitting your knees - strengthen your spirit man so you can carry this load.

Hope breeds eternal misery: Living in ideals is another way to cope. Anchor yourself to a new promise, a promise from God. You anchored yourself to your pimp's promises for far too long.

Structure: Most of us see structure and submission as someone trying to control us, and we instantly want to rebel. The structure births freedom in the spiritual realm. We need structure to keep us safe, to help us learn to make wise decisions and to teach us that being "normal" is not only obtainable but enjoyable!

My pastor's wife told me once to think of submission as if you are submitting a resume for a job. In a resume, we highlight the most attractive, impressive qualities that we possess and hope they choose us. When we submit our will to our authorities, we are submitting our best and trusting that the outcome is the most suited for our situation. It is not a matter of who controls who; it is a matter of God knowing what is best for us even after our "authority" reviews our suggestions.

Vicarious Drama: do you find yourself caught in drama several times throughout the year? Maybe you need to take some time to reflect on the fact that "drama" has become comfortable and familiar to you. However, it's toxic and will lead to broken relationships and reputations you don't want. Catch yourself when starting to engage in drama, in gossip, in thinking of the worst of someone else's intentions. Keep your thoughts on things above and stay out of the mess.

Which "boundary pangs" can you identify with?

_____
_____
_____
_____

Are you prepared to deal with your boundary pangs so that you can have a better looking future?

_____

So now that we have a real grasp on what trafficking looks like and we've come out of denial, are you ready to move onto part two? Be encouraged- your garden is almost weeded! We can begin filling in those holes with soil from the Holy Spirit. We can plant and fertilize fruit that will be juicy and sweet. Your garden is looking beautiful. You can do this!! You were born for greatness!

I encourage you to take some time to get into the Word before Part Two. The story of Esther can be found in the Old Testament. It is only seven chapters, so think of it as a short story. Esther was an amazing woman who despite her circumstances, stepped out in faith to save her people.  The latter part of Esther 4:14 is a much-quoted scripture: "…perhaps you were made queen for such a time as this?"

I hope you read her story and allow it to minister to where you are in your life today.

# Part II – Pathway to Hope
## Mentoring Survivors: Assisting victims at any stage of recovery

# INTRODUCTION

The science of Neurophysiology has shown that there are actual, physical connections in our brains that form as we create habits.  Each time we choose a certain area, a pathway in our brain forms.  I know there are much more technical terms for all of this, but I'm trying to paraphrase simply here, so bear with me.

Consider the example of pioneering a new piece of land.  After a "trail" has been traveled so many times, it becomes visible.  If we were in the early stages of community development, eventually the city roads department would come in and pave that trail and turn it into an actual road.  Our brains do the same thing.  The more we choose to travel a neuropathy or "road" the more it becomes a permanent pathway in our brains: a sort of "second nature" habit.

If the "city" wanted to get rid of a road and create a new, better way, then they would call in the construction crew.  When construction takes place, they block the exit and reroute traffic.  We need to do the same with our brains.  If the exit to our neuro-pathway is closed off long enough, our brains will use a new route.  Then, after enough use, we have a new visible path or "trail" that our construction crew can come in and turn into a road.  The old pathway is no longer used, and our new route has become our new "second nature."

Part Two is all about finding the unacceptable paths in our minds, setting up roadblocks, making a detour and then building those new, paths into paved roads.  You may be tired of all my analogies to the physical realm, but they help so much in painting a clear picture for us to understand. So, I'm going to give you one more:

Just like driving on a dirt road can be difficult, so can creating that new path and using it enough to form a visible trail. It's bumpy and rough and uncomfortable. But don't give up!!! Turning unchartered mountains into trails and then paved roads can be an adventure. And afterward, you have an amazing city that you can be proud of!

# CHAPTER FIVE:

———————————————

## Mentoring Survivors: Assisting victims at any stage of recovery

I think by now you can identify with the word "victim" or "survivor" rather than just a prostituted person. I'm so proud of you for breaking those myths that you've believed for far too long. So how do we move forward to become "overcomers" as my friend Pastor Sean Wrench puts it?

Bonding

If you are seeking recovery from the "sex industry" you probably are surrounded by several people trying to help you reach your full potential. Service providers, counselors, mentors, other survivors, family, and friends are all trying to help keep you on the path to success.

However, if you are anything like me, and I am guessing we're VERY much alike, we do not make it easy on them.

When my family first took my daughter because of my drug addiction, they handed me a list of recovery shelters and told me I couldn't have her back until I got clean. They didn't know at the time, about the trafficking. All they saw was a drug addict mother and a hungry little girl.

I looked at their list and saw a Christian woman's home along with a handful of other secular programs.

"These Christians ain't got a clue what my life is like," I told my mother and rolled my eyes. I called every other shelter on the list except the Christian facility. God knew what He was doing though, and no shelter had vacancy except the house of God!

You can imagine my dismay when I pulled into the women's home and was greeted by an older man, about my father's age with a gruff, Latino exterior and a tattoo on his neck. "Are you Sister Rebecca from Vegas?" He asked.

It was my home director Pastor Joseph Islas. It is interesting how God always knows exactly what will get and keep our attention. I thought to myself, "ok, homeboy is alright, if this how Christians are, maybe I can stay for a little while."

So, what can you expect in treatment? Whether you are in a shelter or living at home, or maybe you are still in your own apartment or some form of transitional housing, God has brought lots of different people in your life to surround you.

We all form different types of bonds with different types of people. Girlfriend, this is for our benefit! God brings some people into our lives to water, some to uproot, some to plant, or some to tear down those walls we've built up. Here are a couple of examples of different types of people that God will bring into your life for this season. In the margin, jot down the name(s) of the person(s) in your life that currently fits each role.

Hatchet: This person, while sometimes we think is mean or bitter, is crucial to our success. It is vital as survivors, to have healthy structure and boundaries. In the beginning, we do not even know what those look like- especially if we were raised in a home without them. A hatchet wants you to become more than just what your parents were. They will enforce rules and call you on your crap sometimes. It may be hard, but it's important. Remember, wounds from a friend are better than kisses from an enemy (Proverbs 27:6)

Friend: Sometimes it is hard for our friend also to be our hatchet, but not impossible. This person will encourage and build you up. They love you, even if it is hard to imagine someone loving you and not wanting anything in return. A friend DOES want something in exchange for their love though: they want YOUR love. When you are feeling discouraged or downtrodden, your friend will come along side and cheer you on. They truly want to see you reach your full potential in Christ.

Mentor: This is someone who will walk you through situations that you can't figure out on your own. Let's face it; our thought process got us to where we were in the first place, so we desperately need to change the way our mind works! Mentors help us with that. They sometimes, but not always, have walked the road we've been on and can help show you the way out.

Different Survivors: Other women who have been through what you've been through are so great to be surrounded with. There are many online survivor network groups that I encourage you to seek out. People in this world do not have the same types of issues as we have. Having an opening to discuss real topics with others who can identify makes you feel more "normal." Don't hide what happened to you or down play or stuff it in. Other healthy survivors will not be shocked by your feelings, thoughts or testimony. If you do not have a friend, mentor or hatchet in your life, I guarantee you can find one among these other amazing survivors.

Mentors do not need to be survivors, and the mentors in your life should change as your walk with the Lord strengthens and as your development and goals find new levels of accomplishments.

Now that I feel healed enough from trafficking to move into ministry, I still need mentors in my life. I tend to seek out mentors that reflect what I would like to become as a healthy Christian woman. I see a gracious woman in the church that handles conflict with a softly spoken word, and I'll ask her to go to coffee and pick her brain. Being teachable is crucial to your success. Growing never ends, so with each step in your walk, find a suitable mentor.

All of these types of people are only human too. Remember that! No one is perfect and if you put too much confidence in them, when they fall short, and oh will they, you will be left disappointed and hurt. Let the people in your life be human. Mentors have disagreements with their spouses- they have just learned how to do it in a non-violent, healthy manner. Friends get frustrated with their children sometimes- but they have learned how to pray through it and respond kindly even when they don't "feel" like it. Hatchets are not always hard, allow them to be kind and loving toward the waitress without wondering why they don't treat you that way. Be careful not to judge or think of them as hypocrites. We ALL have things that we're working on, including them.

Be yourself and be honest with people that are trying to pour into you. You have to get close enough with these people to catch their disease if you want to change.

Iron Sharpens Iron

"As iron sharpens iron, so one person sharpens another." - Proverbs 27:17

Life is surrounded with people, it's just how it is. Real life interaction will prepare us for the real world. We must learn healthy interaction. How do you think God teaches us to interact with people?

_____

_____

In school, we may have attended a math class, read through the lesson book and listened to the teacher in front instruct us. In your Christian walk, this is not necessarily the case.

Yes, God gives us a lesson book: THE BIBLE. However, He then allows situations to arise in our lives to sharpen us, to teach us, and to allow us to practice. Think of that as God giving you homework.

When we are ready, we will be faced with people that challenge us. They have their own agendas, their own struggles, their own hang ups, etc. What are we going to do the first time one of them rubs us the wrong way? This is God's way of giving you a pop quiz.

_____

_____

Are we going to throw in the towel, cuss them out and call our pimp and go back to be hardened and callused? (your answer here should be NO) _____

What if you are convinced NOT to go back to your pimp, but the person who just rubbed you the wrong way is in your church?

Will you pack up and move to a different church? (again, your answer here should be NO) _____

Will you forsake this whole "Christian" thing and decide to just be normal? _____

Satan would love for you just to be normal. So, what if he lost a team member who used to play for the game? As long as you are not playing for God's team, he is not worried about you.

"When Pharaoh finally let the people go, God did not lead them along the main road that runs through Philistine territory, even though that was the shortest route to the Promised Land. God said, "If the people are faced with a battle, they might change their minds and return to Egypt." - Exodus 13:17 (NLT)

So why do we need to learn these lessons?

We must learn how to interact with the tyrant of a boss if we want to keep our jobs. We must learn how to listen and learn from that annoying teacher if we want to pass that class. We must learn how not to get offended when a co-worker says something inappropriate if we want to keep the peace.

Turn with me to 2 Timothy 1:7. "For God has not given us a spirit of fear, but of power and love and _____."

Self-Control, beloved, is one of those words I use to cringe when hearing. I won't lie, sometimes I still do cringe. But I have learned over the years that when I feel like lashing out and telling everyone what's really on my mind, I hit my knees! Not every time, but most times.

No one can change that person's heart or your own but God. Tell Him about it and watch your faith be built up as He diffuses the situation without you having to say a thing!

I spoke at an event recently, and when I got home, I went on my social media site to check my newsfeed. I saw someone post on our fan page a comment about the event that I took offense to. I knew this was probably not the person's intentions, so I left it alone. It ate and ate and ate at me all through the night. Finally, I just said a quick prayer about it asking God to show that person the truth. The next morning, I went back on again to catch up with any other news and low and behold, that person corrected themselves!

"Maybe I should be clearer..." they started. Haha, isn't God good?

We cannot play Holy Spirit in people's lives. So, learn to take everything to Him, and He will work it out.

Can you think of a situation right now that someone is bothering, annoying or offending you? Instead of responding impulsively, pray about whether the situation is trying to show you that you may have a weed hiding in your heart:

_____

_____

_____

_____

_____

_____

_____

_____

_____

_____

_____

_____

_____

_____

_____

"And we know that all things work together for good to those who love God, to those who are the called according to His purpose." -Romans 8:28

Having a roommate in a shelter is hard, having a difficult Home Director is hard, having a snotty assigned Mentor is hard. TRUST that God has a plan and He may be preparing you for that season in the future when you may have a difficult teacher, boss or in-laws. You may feel like cussing out your roommate, but that is not a healthy response. God will allow you opportunities to learn how to handle situations in a Godly manner… And if you don't pass don't worry! God is not mad at you. He loves you so much that He'll give you another opportunity to try again ;) What a great teacher.

Breathing Purpose and Value

You may or may not remember from Sunday School as a little girl, but we tend to hear lots of stories in the Bible like Noah and the Ark, Daniel and the lion's den, Adam and Eve. We rarely hear about Rahab the prostitute and brothel owner that was such a smart business woman, she had her house of harlotry right near the gates of Jericho, so no matter who came or went, they passed her! We rarely hear about Paul, the apostle who wrote the majority of the New Testament while on HOUSE ARREST or locked up in jail.

Surprisingly enough, God used people like you and me, like Rahab and Paul to change generations. God's army hid away in Rahab's brothel while they were scouting out the land, and because of that, God spared her and her family, and she ended up in the lineage of Jesus Christ! Paul turned

Christianity upside down because of his "Damascus Road Experience."

Familiarize yourself with stories in the bible like these. Once you see how God sees people like you and me, then you will feel truly valued! He wants to you use you too.

Story of Rahab can be found in Joshua Chapter 2
The life of Paul can be read in the book of Acts

There seems to be a victim mentality that I have seen creep into women who have suffered trauma. The attention they get from being the victim is what they desire, but it isn't healthy. The Bible tells us to be free and sin no more. (John 8:11)

There is a difference between "stuffing the trauma" and grieving then letting go.  It may seem like a fine line, but one allows you to move on, and one keeps you in bondage.

Do not take on a victim role - focus on your future and let your mind stay busy with what you WANT to become, not who you USE to be.

- Be aware of your negative thoughts
- Practice affirmations
- Turn mistakes into lessons

Sometimes being "Christian" can feel as if there are a whole new set of rules that we come under.  We swap out one set of rules of the life in for a set of rules for the church.  While the enemy wants you to believe that, it is not the truth.

A lot of girls who first leave the sex industry can become extreme in their behaviors.  They have not felt freedom for so long, that it is invigorating to shop for whatever YOU want for the first time, eat at the restaurant YOU want to eat at, even go on a couple of meaningless dates with normal guys.

All of this behavior is normal. It is exciting to figure out your own interests and likes for the first time in years. However, you must know that the ONLY freedom comes from serving Christ. Otherwise, you're just swapping one bondage for another: trafficking for idolatry to money, or addiction to being in love. Any road that leads you away from Jesus is slavery. Recognize when you are going too far down that "freedom" road and get back on track quickly!!

"Not everyone who says to me, 'Lord, Lord,' will enter the kingdom of heaven, but only the one who does the will of my Father who is in heaven. Many will say to me on that day, 'Lord, Lord, did we not prophesy in your name and in your name, drive out demons and in your name, perform many miracles?' Then I will tell them plainly, 'I never knew you. Away from me, you evildoers!' "- Matthew 7:21-23

That word "knew" in Greek is **ginosko** and it is the Jewish idiom for sexual intercourse between a man and a woman. It spoke of intimacy. God is saying, "you've said or done a lot of things: groups, bible studies, classes, Sunday service, home group, but do you know me? Are you intimate with me?" That is only a question you would know that answer too. He desires a relationship with you. You are precious to Him. He wants to be intimate, like a husband and wife.

Share your fears:

_____

Share your dreams:

_____

Although the omniscient Lord and Savior Jesus Christ knows it all.... He desires conversations and relationships with you.

Song of Solomon 1:2 Let him kiss me with the kisses of his mouth— for your love is more delightful than wine. (NIV)
Song of Solomon 2:16 My lover is mine, and I am his. (NLT)
Song of Solomon 4:10 How delightful is your love, my sister, my bride! How much more pleasing is your love than wine and the fragrance of your perfume than any spice! (NIV)
Song of Solomon 8:6 Place me like a seal over your heart, like a seal on your arm; for love is as strong as death, its jealousy unyielding as the grave. It burns like blazing fire, like a mighty flame. (NIV)
Song of Solomon 8:7 Many waters cannot quench love; rivers cannot wash it away. If one were to give all the wealth of his house for love, it would be utterly scorned. (NIV)

### Journal Exercise: My Questions about My Self-Esteem
(taken from The PTSD Workbook)

In a journal or notebook, answer the following questions as fully as you like.

What do I like or value about myself?
What do I do to take care of myself (my body)?
How do I take care of myself emotionally?
What do I do to reward myself, and when and how do I do it?
When and how do I devalue myself or cut myself down?
What are my hopes and dreams?
What are my realistic expectations of myself?
What are my unrealistic expectations of myself?
In what situations do I have a sense of humor?
When and how do I show love and affection?
Where do I find hope?
Under what circumstances am I open and honest about my feelings?
Do I help others feel good about themselves even when I feel bad about myself?

What does God like about me? What is His favorite part of you?

All of the qualities listed above are things God adores about you.

## Finding Skills: What Was I Created to Do?

So, what lured us out of our homes in the first place? Whether it was freedom from an unhealthy home, financial security, excitement or someone to love us, we were all willing to risk our lives for that dream.

My third and final pimp was the most abusive and the one I lived with the longest. I found out later that he had told some of my other "sisters" that I had the type of spirit that needed to be broken.

Why would I stay with him the longest if he was the one whom I had experienced so much violence from? Well, other than the obvious which is straight fear…. He showed glimpses of the future that I always longed to have.

He had a beautiful home and nice cars. My daughter attended private school. He would arrive at all her school activities and events and put on the facade that we had a perfectly happy home. I assumed that due to his size and our financial success, most people thought I was married to an NFL player or something… It seemed from the outside as if we had it all.

My other "sisters" had wanted kids with our man, and he either made them have abortions or beat them until they miscarried. He told me I was different. He told me that he wanted to have a family with me. He even took me to the doctor so we could start planning. He made me go to one of my sister's homes and tell her face to face that we were going

94

to have a baby. All of that was an actual game to him - he kept that carrot dangling close enough to my face to think it was only a short time away. It also was his attempt to pit us against each other.

This lie that I wanted so badly to be the truth, was the hope I anchored myself to when times became severe. Can you think of a lie that your pimp told you that kept you from running during hard times? Can you think of a situation that may not have been voiced out loud but a scenario that you longed to have with this man?_____

_____
_____
_____
_____
_____
_____
_____
_____
_____
_____
_____
_____
_____
_____

So how can we move on? How can we just forget the dream that we thought was so close (even if it NEVER actually was)?

This is the best part of the work book! We are going to create a new dream, a new "roadmap" for your future! You will want to share this part of the section with your friends, mentor, hatchets, counselors, family and everyone else in between. The more people you have who know about your new plan means the more people you have around you who can hold you to it. It is called accountability beloved. Do not get mad or angry at them when they call you out for slipping off the path. Be grateful for the "guard rails."

You can take out a blank piece of paper and write the answers to the questions below, you can also get a poster board after praying and answering the questions and make it a collage. It can be fun. We would hang these in our rooms, above our bed or desk to remind us of the NEW dreams that we are anchoring ourselves to when troubles come our way.

Let's pray before we get started:

Lord, thank you so much for this opportunity to help this lady that sits before you. I pray God that you would speak to her heart. Right now, Holy Spirit I believe that you already have planned each person whose hands this workbook would reach. This is a Holy Spirit ordained appointment by God, and we pray for your presence to fall from heaven. Let your train fill this temple that sits before you. Give her insight and wisdom into her future. Help her to see the incredible future that you have for her. Give her hope that she was born for such a time as this and that your plans for her are to prosper her. Let her not lean on her own understanding of how the plan will unfold but that she would trust in you with all her heart.
In Jesus mighty name,
Amen.

Do you already have an idea of what God wants to do with your life? Have you had any promises or prophetic words spoken over you? Write them down.

When you were little, what did you want to be when you grew up? _____

_____

_____

Are there certain things that spark a flame in your heart when you hear about them now?  You can't stop thinking about them when you hear about it?  I remember hearing the word "nations" spoken from the pulpit and something inside my chest just wanted to jump up and say "yes!! me!!"  I had no clue what that would look like, but in this space, if I were doing this with you (and beloved I have), I'd write: NATIONS.  What words stand out to you?

_____

_____

_____

_____

You need to know right here and now that WHATEVER God calls you to do is elaborate, amazing and special. Whether that is working at a salon and making women feel beautiful, or in a hospital and caring for the sick.  Whether you're called to ministry and want to build homes in third world countries: ALL callings are significant to the Lord. And let me tell you, being a wife and mother is the greatest calling.  To know that God would entrust us with other men and women of God and believe that WE could have a part in raising them to become those amazing people is unbelievable, isn't it?

Let's create a dream board and roadmap for your future now that you've had a little time to brainstorm.  This dream board can always be added to.  Don't worry it does not have to be the finished goal.

Also, shoot big!  God wants us to have faith that He can do the amazing.  Our belief in Him is what fans our faith into action.

97

If your resources (both time and money) were UNLIMITED, what would you do?

_____
_____
_____
_____

(You know God, your father owns cattle on a thousand hills, right? His resources ARE unlimited. Psalms 50:10)

So, what do you think God wants to do with your life:

_____
_____
_____
_____

When I created my dream board, I wanted to be married with kids; I wanted to be an author of a book that would help others someday, somehow in some capacity, I wanted to preach to the nations and felt that God would call me to travel speaking. I can sit here before you my dear friend and tell you that ALL that I put on my dream board has come to pass AND MORE!!!

DREAMS GOD WANTS YOU TO ACCOMPLISH:

1.
2.
3.
4.
5.

Do you need to go back and add some things to yours? Don't be shy with God. He knows what you are thinking anyway, so there isn't any point in hiding it from Him. If you have the ability to draw pictures, cut things out of magazines, etc. then do so…. Glue it to a journal or poster board and look at it daily.

You need to change your dream from old to new, and you need to put your trust in the only man that will never disappoint you: Jesus!

Can you create a plan of action now on how you will obtain some of those ideas?  Do you need to put college down on that list?  Do you need to put completing your GED on that list?  How about just building a resume?  Talk with your mentors at this time at helping you create a PLAN OF ACTION to accomplish these new dreams.  Can you think of some actions you will need to take to achieve your dreams?

1.
2.
3.
4.
5.

ASK THE PEOPLE THAT ARE POURING INTO YOUR LIFE TO HOLD YOU ACCOUNTABLE AND KEEP YOU ON THAT TRACK.

It can be easy to forget the motivation behind the desire to change.  We need to be reminded of what we are fighting for. This is the time when the path is rocky, and we're making it a trail, don't give up when bumps come.

Sometimes trying to figure out the path is not easy.  What happens if you do not get approved for financial aid for school?  Knock on another door!  What happens if God hasn't opened a door for ministry within the year?  Keep serving; it is coming.

Do you remember the same tenacity that you use to go after money with? You would go on call after call, jumping in car after car. You did not let the NO's discourage you. Let God use that drive you were born with to go after His promises too!

"IT IS EASY TO CHOOSE THE GAME, IT TAKES A STRONG PERSON TO CHOOSE TO DO THE RIGHT THING!"

Need a tip to pick a path? In the margin, write down the options you have before you. Now, below each option, write down what will happen one month from now if you choose that option, one year from now and three years from now. Seeing it from the end perspective sometimes makes it easier to decide which path to take.

Here is my example. I had started a business with my husband, and after two years it was not thriving- we broke even monthly. I prayed and prayed but did not feel a response. My choices were to sell it, keep it or let it go. I then listed what would happen one month, one year and three years from now if I chose each path. If I were doing this with you right now, here is what the margin of my workbook would look like:

1. **Sell It:**
   - One Month: Walk away out of debt and be free for ministry.
   - One Year: Going after my calling.
   - Three Years: Thankful for the lessons learned, but enjoying my kids and ministry.
2. **Keep It:**
   - One Month: Continue to pay month to month even though times are tough and stay stressed over being stretched so thin between family, work, and ministry.

- One Year: Possibly have it shut down and go into debt and ruin our credit, / or have it pick up and become successful and have no time for ministry.
- Three Years: Working hard to get out of debt and feel terrible about my business not working / or continue to be a business woman and no more ministry and no more children.

3.    **Let it go:**
   - One Month: Put my family 20k in debt instantly.
   - One Year: working to get out of debt.
   - Three Years: Unable to be approved for any loans for any future endeavors.

Sounds like a pretty easy choice when I break it down that simply doesn't it?  I put it up for sale immediately after making this list; because my heart has always been for ministry.

John 10: 17: "The Father loves me because I lay down my life that I may have it back again."

Romans 8:18-19 "Yet, what we suffer now is nothing compared to the glory he will give us later.  For all creation is waiting eagerly for that future day when God will reveal who his children are."

Hosea 4:6 "My people perish for lack of knowledge."

Let us not perish Lord, but give us knowledge that we can continue on the path you put before us.

"The Lord God is my strength, and he has made my feet like hinds feet, and makes me walk on my high places."
(Habakkuk 3:19 and also found in Psalm 18:33)

Here is a little nugget from Hannah's Cupboard about Hinds Feet:

"You have discovered this little cubby hole inside The Cupboard. Now that you are here I want to tell you about the secret of the hinds' feet.

The hind is a female red deer whose home is the mountains. The rear feet of the hind step in precisely the same spot where the front feet have just been. Every motion of the hind is followed through with single-focused consistency, making it the most sure-footed of all mountain animals.

Now listen to how the Lord compares our spiritual walk with the hind..."The Lord God is my strength, and he has made my feet like hinds' feet, and makes me walk on my high places." (Habakkuk 3:19 and also found in Psalm 18:33)

Do you know that the Lord has some high places for you? Places where the air is pure, the view pristine, distractions are far below, and there are paths just big enough for the two of you. It's true that the climb to the high places is a bit more challenging than a level foot path in the valley. But not if you've got those hinds' feet; the hinds' feet equip you for the roughest terrain.
Can't you just smell that mountain air? What are you waiting for?"

# CHAPTER SIX

---

## Undoing the Brainwash

Up until now, the way our minds work has only got us into trouble. This is one of the most important parts of restoration. I'm not talking about victim blaming. Of course, it's not your fault for being abused. What I am referring to is self-awareness. Admitting to yourself that the way you think, the habits you've developed aren't the healthiest. That is NOT your fault. It's not your fault that your childhood impacted the way you see relationships. But it also means that the way you see relationships may not be healthy. Being exposed to criminal activity may have created some habits in your brain that have desensitized to answering questions honestly for example. When caught lying on a job application that could lead to termination. We need to become self-aware of some our habits that have got us into the consequences we walk in today, make sense? Sorry if this insult or offends you, but it's the truth. You need this part to sink in beloved: the way you think only got you into trouble - YOU MUST CHANGE YOUR MINDSET. Pray before you begin, for a teachable spirit to be released from Heaven, that God will open your heart and mind to receive this next bit of information.

### The Building Process

Girls in the game, or the life, have been brainwashed to think that only "suckers" leave their pimps; "weak women who run when things get tough." It is important to know that you ARE valuable; you ARE making the right decision, you ARE strong, and you ARE born for a purpose.

"Sarah" used to be the girl in her pimp's home that showed the new girls how to work. He trusted her to train the new "ho" on how to get money, how to be with tricks, how to get out of dangerous situations, etc. This made her feel special. She took her role as "bottom" very seriously. When she came into recovery, she fell immediately into her old patterns and took it upon herself to "show" some of the other girls how things were ran in the recovery home.

"Jenny" used to be trafficked through pornography. When she finally was able to exit and went through a recovery program, she emerged ready to be a public speaker. However, her methods came across as very "book me, here's my headshot" just like she used to do to book a film. It made people uncomfortable because *THEY* could sense a lack of healing that Jenny didn't understand. You see habits sometimes need to be addressed and changed through self-awareness. I challenged Jenny to take 30 days off from pursuing bookings, to allow God to open doors and start to create new habits of patience and trust in God.

Identifying old behaviors and redirecting is crucial to your success! You also need to know that when the Holy Spirit brings something to the light that needs to be changed, DO NOT condemn yourself. God does not expect perfection, and He is NOT waiting over you with a stick so he can get you in trouble. He is the one showing you the weed so you can pull it!

In Sarah's instance, while explaining to a new girl the ins and outs of a group home may seem harmless, it is the old behavior rising to the surface that needs to be redirected.

Taking nightly inventory is a great way to sift through old behaviors. At the end of the day, ask the Holy Spirit to reveal the answers to the questions below. Let's go ahead and do one now just so we can get the hang of it:

Has anything happened today that made you think of your past? _____

_____

_____

_____

_____

_____

Has anything happen today that made you feel upset, angry or anxious? _____

_____

_____

_____

_____

I was working with two women last week who both had been trafficked by the same pimp. One was now working, sharing an apartment with a roommate. The other at home with her parents and newborn baby, attending college. The woman with the roommate called me needing prayer:

"My roommate came home and went to her room and shut the door. She didn't speak to me. I'm sick to my stomach thinking I did something to upset her. I've been racking my brain about what I could have done; left the clothes in the dryer? Dishes in the sink?"

A couple of days later, I called the new mother to talk to her about this very workbook (follow me, I'll bring the connection between each story in a minute).

I told the new mother that I had something to ask her. I proceeded to ask her to go through this work book and give me her honest feedback. She started laughing.

"I thought you were mad at me and I was in trouble for something. I was going through my mind trying to think if there was anything I did or said to offend you..."

Do you see how both of these women from the same trafficked "home" agonized over being in trouble? The severe abuse they both suffered at the hands of their abuser made them constantly live in fear. If left unattended, this can breed a sort of "perfectionist" spirit that is equally as unhealthy in normal relationships.

Here's a prayer I often say when I find something in my life that needs to be fixed. Go ahead and read it, then rewrite it in the space provided filling in your own blanks. This sort of dual processing (reading and writing) helps our brain retain information better:

Heavenly Father, bind the spirit of insecurity and fear from my heart in Jesus name (fill in the blank with whatever area you desire to get rid of). Pull it like a weed, Lord! Insecurity and Fear have no place here and no longer have dominion over my life. Holy Spirit, please come and replace that area in my heart with security and courage (put the name of the opposite trait here). Thank you, Lord for softening the soil before you rip the root out. In the name of your Son Jesus, Amen.

Write this prayer here, with your undesired traits, in the space provided:

---------------------------------------------------------------
---------------------------------------------------------------
---------------------------------------------------------------
---------------------------------------------------------------
---------------------------------------------------------------
---------------------------------------------------------------
---------------------------------------------------------------
---------------------------------------------------------------
---------------------------------------------------------------
---------------------------------------------------------------
---------------------------------------------------------------
---------------------------------------------------------------
---------------------------------------------------------------
---------------------------------------------------------------
---------------------------------------------------------------

So how do we recognize those behaviors? How do we even see when a weed needs pulled?

Our hearts can be like an onion: we have many, many layers. God does not always go right for the center. It is a process that can take time. I have had girls ask me why things come up after they've given their lives to the Lord. Usually, it's because we need to heal from the issues that made us vulnerable to that trafficker in the first place.

Look at this onion diagram:

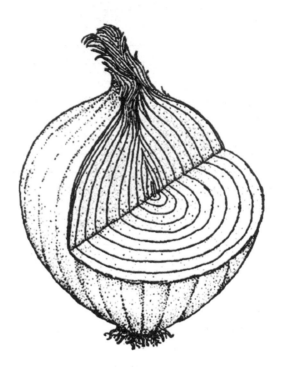

My onion may have layers that work their way from the outer
layer in toward the center like this:

- Outer Layer: Being Mean
- Next Layer: Abuse from my pimp
- Next: Heartbreak from him
- Next: Desperate to find a family for my baby
- Deeper Layer: Getting teased in school
- Deeper: My dad leaving me in the car so he could go
  in the bar
- Almost to the core: My mom almost getting drowned
  in the bath tub by her boyfriend

- Core issue in my heart: Feeling unimportant to my parents because they were busy partying and fighting

Why don't you take some time to label your onion above?

Now, go through each layer with Jesus.

Ask Him: "Show me, Jesus, where you were in that situation."
After He has shown you and you have talked to Him about how each incident made you feel, pray our prayer we just went through on the last page. Fill in the blank again with what you want to be removed and then ask the Holy Spirit to fill that hole with the opposite.

"Ask, and it will be given to you; seek, and you will find; knock, and it will be opened to you. For everyone who asks receives, and he who seeks finds, and to him who knocks it will be opened. Or what man is there among you who, if his son asks for bread, will give him a stone? Or if he asks for a fish, will he give him a serpent? If you then, being evil, know how to give good gifts to your children, how much more will your Father who is in heaven give good things to those who ask Him! Therefore, whatever you want men to do to you, do also to them, for this is the Law and the Prophets. - Matthew 7:7-12 (NKJV)

## *It's Healthy to Recognize Unhealth*

Sometimes seeing the issues in each of us can be devastating. We start to feel as if the job is too big. "We rather feel the pain that's all too familiar than be broken by a lover we don't understand." (Jars of Clay: Love of a Jealous Kind)

Realizing how much work we have to do or how far from "perfect" we are, can destroy our self-worth. Remember that you are doing great- it may not feel like it, but it is

HEALTHY to recognize your unhealthy. Right when you feel like, "man I'm awful" try to stop and tell yourself, "You know a little while back I wouldn't have even noticed that was an issue. I have come a long way to recognize that unhealthy behavior!" Celebrate the process.

Most victims have been beaten down physically, verbally, emotionally and sexually for so long, that they already have a very poor impression of themselves. All of our crazy, outrageous behaviors are just coping mechanisms for how we see ourselves. Get out of the habit of beating yourself up, because God surely isn't!

I used to be called a real "b*%@h" because I was mean. I didn't take any b.s. from anyone and me, and my "sisters" would shut girls up real quick if they even mentioned another man's name in our presence. That's because I was hardened and jaded – you have to be to make it in the streets. That sort of behavior and mentality followed me into Christianity. I have worked tirelessly to change that in me- God tells me that I'm a different B word now: Bold. I like that!

Don't be embarrassed to cry out to God about areas in your life that are not who you want to be, and God never intended to be you.

Are there any characteristics in your life that you want to change? _____
_____
_____

Do you have any insecurities about yourself?
_____
_____

Another part of the brainwashing that occurs when you have been trafficked is living with the rules of the game for years. You begin to take on the character traits of your abuser and the requirements he has in the home.

Let me give you another example:

In our home, for example, we were taught that everyone was out to get us, and we could only trust each other. Everyone else, including squares, wanted something from us. We treated the waiter at the restaurant with disrespect if he smiled and asked how our night was. We didn't care if he was friendly because he wanted a tip- we had to make sure not to let him think he could get over on us.

We never turned our heads when another P.I. hollered at us or honked his car horn. If a nice car drove by playing loud music and we turned to look, we were usually beat upside the head for being "out of pocket." We followed the rules.

Now that we are out of the game, once again, we don't get amnesia and all the sudden start acting differently. I still never turn my head in the grocery store when someone is trying to get my attention, even if it just someone from church wanting to say hi. People from church will say, "I've been calling your name." I have to laugh at myself because that it is such an ingrained behavior not to turn and look either that or it took me a long time to be called by my real name.

Can you list some rules you had in your home that you still have not broken the habit of?

_____

_____

_____

Some of you may have tattoos or "brandings" of your pimp's name, his initials or his sayings. But traffickers can use different forms of "branding" too. Did he ever have you wear certain bracelets or rings to prove you were just his? This sort of psychological manipulation and control has just as many triggers as a tattoo. List some of these constant reminders that he/she put on you:

_____

_____

_____


Certain words can also have a negative connotation that God wants desperately to redeem in us. When I first came to Christ, I would hear women pray out loud at bible studies, or prayer meetings and anytime they asked, "daddy God" to do something, I cringed inside.

I found so much disgust in the word "daddy" from pimps calling themselves that, but God did not intend for such an endearing term to be tainted.

Are there certain words that make your skin crawl that you believe God wants to redeem?

_____

_____

_____

_____

_____

_____

_____


When I first started dating my now husband, whom I met in church, he would tell me that I was beautiful. I'd get upset with him because that word made me think he wanted something from me. I used to hear that from tricks and pimps. I'd ask him not to call me that, but to find things on the inside that he liked about me. I loved his response, "I'm going to redeem that word for you in Jesus name." Boy am I thankful that God brought someone into my life who was up for a challenge!

I think we need some fresh manna right now: Here is a passage from Romans 8: 31-39 (NLT)

### Nothing Can Separate Us from God's Love

"What shall we say about such wonderful things as these? If God is for us, who can ever be against us? Since he did not spare even his own Son but gave him up for us all, won't he also give us everything else? Who dares accuse us whom God has chosen for his own? No one—for God himself has given us right standing with himself. Who then will condemn us? No one—for Christ Jesus died for us and was raised to life for us, and he is sitting in the place of honor at God's right hand, pleading for us.

Can anything ever separate us from Christ's love? Does it mean he no longer loves us if we have trouble or calamity, or are persecuted, or hungry, or destitute, or in danger, or threatened with death? (As the Scriptures say, "For your sake, we are killed every day; we are being slaughtered like sheep.") No, despite all these things, overwhelming victory is ours through Christ, who loved us.

And I am convinced that nothing can ever separate us from God's love. Neither death nor life, neither angels nor demons, neither our fears for today nor our worries about tomorrow—not even the powers of hell can separate us from God's love. No power in the sky above or in the earth below—indeed, nothing in all creation will ever be able to separate us from the love of God that is revealed in Christ Jesus our Lord."

## Bacteria Grows in the Dark

113

Negative thoughts are like mold in our minds. They grow in dark places.

We MUST talk about the lies that are going on in our minds- these negative thoughts are just like playing teeter-totter on the playground with Satan. Why entertain him?

Every time I used to speak at an engagement, I would drive home and the thought, "no one will believe you, it wasn't that bad" would continually play in my mind. It was not until my first trip to another state to mentor a trafficked woman did I finally see the lie. Her ex-pimp had texted her trying to get her to come back while I was there. He used that exact statement "it wasn't that bad," and it hit me! I heard an old voice myself! My pimp used to say that to me after a beating, "no one will believe you. It wasn't that bad". Even after all these years, his lies continued to linger in my own thought life.

So how do we change that thought into the opposite? Start speaking OUT LOUD, the complete opposite, even if you don't believe it… Yet! In my "no one will believe you" scenario, I started saying out loud while driving home: "Getting punched in the stomach until I couldn't breathe was that bad. Telling my daughter that mommy was in car accident because my face was unrecognizable after a beating, WAS that bad."

We need to VALIDATE what we have been through and not discount it or push it under the rug. It will only grow in the dark if we do that!

A great question to ask yourself throughout the day, is "What is going through my mind right now?" If it is pure and holy and brings edification to you, then it is from God. If it is condemning and fearful, then it is not of God, and you need to change the channel to an opposite statement!

114

'There no condemnation to those in Christ Jesus." - Romans 8:1
"For God didn't give us a spirit of fear, but of power, love, and self-control." - 2 Timothy 1:7

Can you list some tips you want to put into practice thus far from Part II? Has there been a statement in the last chapter that has changed your mindset? Write a couple down so we can retain them in our memory a little better:

List three crucial points that will help you pull those weeds?
1.
2.
3.

Don't worry - you can do this! You were born for greatness! No eye has seen, no ear has heard, no mind has imagined the plan that God has for those He loves and are called according to His purpose. If God is for you, who can be against you? Greater is He that is in you than He that is in the world. No weapon formed against you shall prosper. Go boldly to the throne of grace and obtain mercy in this time of need. Let your requests be known and the peace that surpasses all understanding will guard your heart and mind.

I hope and pray that you are getting into your word on a daily basis. Yes, books are good, and I've listed several in the back of the workbook that has helped me tremendously with my growth. But there is nothing that replaces the living word of God.

I know that things can pile up and the stresses of everyday life can consume us. But man cannot live on bread alone; your spiritual body needs to be fed and exercised too if you want it to grow and develop. Draw near to God, and He will draw near to you. There is a war out for your soul, and you are such a mighty woman, the devil wants you DESPERATELY on his team.  Don't let him win!  Our next chapter we'll deal with spiritual warfare, so buckle up cause we're about to learn how to use our swords!

# CHAPTER SEVEN

---

## Lying Devil: Overcoming Spiritual Warfare

"The thief does not come except to steal, and to kill, and to destroy. I have come that they may have life and that they may have it more abundantly." -John 10:10 (NKJV)
"Be alert and of sober mind. Your enemy, the devil, prowls around like a roaring lion looking for someone to devour. Resist him, standing firm in the faith, because you know that the family of believers throughout the world is undergoing the same kind of sufferings." - 1 Peter 5:8 (NIV)
"You are of God, little children, and have overcome them because He who is in you is greater than he who is in the world." - 1 John 4:4

There is a current war in the spiritual realm going on that we cannot see and it is for our souls.  At one point in your life, I would care to bet you were a General for the devil.  You allowed him to control your thoughts, desires, and emotions without realizing that it was him- that's part of his scam.  You did a lot of damage for the kingdom of darkness.  He is not happy that you've switched teams. He is not going to easily let you play for the kingdom of light now. It will be a flat-out war for you. Who will you let win? Darkness or Light?

_____

I don't want to spend this work book trying to convince you of spiritual warfare if you do not believe in it already. There are many great books out there that will use scripture to give you any information on this matter. This work book rather is to equip you with weapons of war on the issues we as survivors of human trafficking experience. So, let's agree that spiritual warfare exists and move onto how to engage in war.

ARMOR
Turn with me to Ephesians 6:10-17

"Finally, be strong in the Lord and his mighty power. Put on the full armor of God, so that you can take your stand against the devil's schemes. For our struggle is not against flesh and blood, but against the rulers, against the authorities, against the powers of this dark world and the spiritual forces of evil in the heavenly realms. Therefore, put on the full armor of God, so that when the day of evil comes, you may be able to stand your ground, and after you have done everything, to stand. Stand firm then, with the belt of truth buckled around your waist, with the breastplate of righteousness in place, and with your feet fitted with the readiness that comes from the gospel of peace. In addition to all this, take up the shield of faith, with which you can extinguish all the flaming arrows of the evil one. Take the helmet of salvation and the sword of the Spirit, which is the word of God."
God gives us armor to help us with our fight. I encourage you to try to memorize each item. Let's list them here:

Belt of _____
Breastplate of _____
Feet fitted in _____

Shield of _____
Helmet of _____
Sword of the _____ (which is the _____ of God)

In the blank area on the right, write each part of your body, in the physical, that those pieces protect. Helmet, for example, protects your brain, right?

Now next to the word "Brain" write what the spiritual synonym is. For this example, next to the brain, we may write: "Mind."

This exercise will help you when you pray the armor of God on each morning to visualize what exactly you are protecting.

Every morning, begin your day by putting on the armor of God. Start from the top and work your way down, visualizing each piece in its rightful place.

FIERY ARROWS

Look at the scripture again, specifically focusing on verse 16: "flaming arrows of the evil one." Can you imagine what that might look like in real life?

I can! When I wake up late is usually the time when my husband is trying to be jovial with me. Instead of taking it that way, however, I snap at him and cause discord in our home. I fell for the fiery arrow that came my way. Instead of extinguishing the arrow with my shield of faith by saying "I have faith that my husband is trying to be funny this morning to make me laugh and that his intention is not to make me annoyed," I let the arrow get me.

EXTINGUISH

That word "extinguish" in other biblical translations is "quench, " and in Greek, it is "*sbennymi*." It means:

- to suppress, stifle

1) of divine influence

In the Webster's dictionary, the word extinguish means
1. to put out (fire, light, etc.); put out the flame of (something burning or lighted): to extinguish a candle.
2. to put an end to or bring to an end; wipe out of existence; annihilate: to extinguish hope.

So how do we extinguish those thoughts that come to our mind? How do we suppress the thoughts, bring an end to the thoughts or wipe them out? I want to give you FIVE weapons that will help you fight, and eventually will form a new path in your brains.

TRUTH
Quote Scripture OUT LOUD- the devil cannot hear your thoughts, he is not as powerful as God. You must audibly counter the lies with truth. Below are some snippets of my favorite truth statements that I have memorized that I will recite when I'm bogged down with thoughts of fear, anger or doubt (I encourage you to look through your word and read the entire verse, rather than my little snippet):

If God is for me, who can be against me? (Romans 8:31)
No weapon formed against me shall prosper. (Isaiah 54:17)
Greater is He that is in me than he that is in the world. (1 John 4:4)
His plans for me are to prosper me not to harm me. (Jer. 29:11)
Nothing can separate his love from me. (Romans 8:38)
He is concerned with what concerns me. (Psalms 138:8)
He doesn't take back His gifts, and He doesn't change His mind! (Romans 11:29, Numbers 23:19)

Do you have any favorites that I haven't mentioned?

_____

_____

_____

2. Praise
God inhabits the praises of His people. (Psalm 22:3
paraphrased)

One afternoon, my family and I were on our way to one of
my speaking engagements.  I felt more anxiety than usual, and
as we got in the car late, my husband started thumbing
through the radio stations before putting the car in reverse.
Inside my mind, I was screaming "hurry the F*%# up!!!"
Those thoughts are not usually how I think, so I recognized
the thought was from Satan immediately.  Instead of
partnering with him and getting anxious over our tardiness, I
refused.  I did the opposite, and I lifted my hands, laid my
head back against the seat and started singing the first praise
song that came to mind as loud as I could.

Instantly peace fell, and the anxiety vanished! Talk about
quenching that arrow.  And surprisingly enough, when I
arrived at the church (on time might I add), there were 4-5
girls from the "at risk youth center" sitting in my front row.
The enemy would have loved to get my husband and I
fighting.  I would have been filled with tension rather than
filled with the Holy Spirit, and my message may not have
been nearly as impactful.

3. Faith Statements
Sometimes I know the scripture, and I am speaking it over
and over again, but the thought still is not leaving.  What do
you do then?  What if you don't quite know your word well
enough to quote scripture yet?

Ever heard the saying "fake it til you make it?" Well, we like to turn that into "faith it til you make it!" Speak the opposite over your situation.

When my husband and I first got married, I struggled with this new role as a Christian wife. I felt like my husband was always mad at me even when he wasn't.

I used to drive and repeat faith statements until I truly believed them: "My husband loves me, and he's on my team. My husband loves me, and he's on my team."

Do you have a thought of negativity running through your mind often? List the opposite here and start repeating it throughout the day:

_____

_____

_____

4. Focus Your Fight
Reread Galatians 6:10-17, but focus specifically on verse 12:

"For our struggle is not against_____ and_____, but against the rulers, against the authorities, against the powers of this dark world and the spiritual forces of evil in the heavenly realms."
When we get offended, upset, angry or hurt, we tend to blame the person. "I don't like her..." , "my boss is so annoying..." , "oh no she didn't...," "she is out of line..."

But, what does scripture say? WE DONT FIGHT AGAINST FLESH AND BLOOD. That means that the enemy has slipped a fiery arrow into your ear and it made its way to your mind. You need to refocus your thoughts and do the opposite. Not always, but usually, I am pretty good at telling myself, "the devil would love for me to get annoyed by that lady because then I won't receive the word she is about to give me."

Rebuke Satan and refocus where your annoyance, frustration or anger should lie: with the demons trying to attack! Do not fight against the flesh and blood that is standing before you, instead remember WHO you fight and rebuke him, sing a praise song or better yet- respond with kindness. He hates that. *This takes a conscious, deliberate choice minute by minute.

5. Take Captive
"For the weapons of our warfare are not carnal but mighty in God for pulling down strongholds, casting down arguments and every high thing that exalts itself against the knowledge of God, bringing every thought into captivity to the obedience of Christ, and being ready to punish all disobedience when your obedience is fulfilled." 2 Corinthians 10:4-6 NKJV

I want you to focus on the latter part of verse 5: BRING EVERY THOUGHT INTO CAPTIVITY TO THE OBEDIENCE OF CHRIST.

What does that mean? When I first got saved, I did not recognize the voice of God very easily. Someone gave me a great analogy that I want to pass onto you.

Your thoughts come from one of three places:
1. Thought from God (that leads to life and can usually be backed up by scripture)
2. Thought from yourself and are just carnal thoughts (what's for dinner, should I stop and get milk, etc.)
3. Thoughts from Satan and demonic influence (these are usually negative and lead to death).

Taking each thought captive, means stopping when your thoughts start to get crazy and saying to yourself, "is this thought from God, Self or Satan?" Then, to make that thought obedient to Christ, you can use one of the first four weapons: Truth, Praise, Faith Statement, Focus your Fight.

So how do we get to know God's voice?

Have you ever met a guy and gave him your number? Of course, you have.

The first time he called, you probably asked, "Who is this?" Even with the advent of caller ID, you didn't recognize the number.

After a while of spending time together, and talking until wee hours of the night, you could recognize his voice anywhere. Because you recognize his voice, his phone could have been lost or stolen, and he could call you from a friend's. Right away you would ask "where are you calling from?"

The same thing goes for God. The more time you spend in prayer and His word, the more you get to know His voice. It becomes easier to differentiate your thoughts from thoughts from God or Satan.

# CHAPTER EIGHT

---

## Triggers: "What sets you off?"

A life of forced prostitution and human trafficking almost always ensures you will suffer from some form or varying degree of post-traumatic stress disorder. We, however, tend to have triggers that differ slightly from someone who may have experienced living through a hurricane for example. The weapons of spiritual warfare that we just learned about are crucial to help diffuse or extinguish triggers!

Sometimes we do not even realize that we have a trigger. It's usually a thought or emotion that floods your mind and body. It is hard to let go of that emotion, and so you lash out usually in an unhealthy manner. Any heightened emotional response is a red flag that you're having a trigger.

We want to help you learn to identify your triggers, or roadblocks on your trail so that you don't fall when you come across one:

Look up Exodus 13: 17 and fill in the blank:

"When Pharaoh finally let the people go, God did not lead them along the main road that runs through Philistine territory, even though that was the shortest route to the Promised Land. God said, "If the people are faced with a battle, they might change their minds and _____.""

Let's do something to make this verse hit home... I've made some space for you below:

Cross out the name Pharaoh and put your trafficker's name there.
Cross out the phrase "the people" and write your name there. Reread it:

"When _____ finally let _____ go, God did not lead her along the main road that runs through the Philistine territory, even though that was the shortest route to the Promised Land. God said, "if _____ is faced with a battle, she might change her mind and return.""

The calling that God has on your life requires a certain amount of faith and perseverance. How do you strengthen a muscle? You work it out; you exercise it. These small triggers are an opportunity to strengthen those muscles. Are you going to drop the weight? Walk away and stay weak? I would care to bet your answer is no because you and I are a lot alike and we want to fight that lying devil and win this war for our souls. We want to take on the challenge to get strong enough to fight him back, because we are tired of him controlling our life and we want more for our future!

Think of triggers as God giving us an opportunity to exercise those Godly characteristics that are going to help us reach our full potential in Christ. Let's list the fruits of the spirit here - these are our spiritual muscles that God wants to strengthen:

You can find them in Galatians 5:22

126

1.

2.

3.

4.

5.

6.

7.

8.

9.

So how do we identify when we have a trigger? Anything that is opposite of the above fruits should be an indicator.

Here are just a couple that tends to come up a lot with women who have experienced sex trafficking:

Money: The addiction to fast money is a hard one to get used to living without. Living on a normal budget is not easy at first, but hundreds of thousands of people do it every month without selling their bodies, and so can you!

Find a local free budgeting class, either with the public library, community college or ask your church if they offer an upcoming Christian budgeting class. Find ways to shop frugally and most important use our prayer example to pray for the addiction of money to be uprooted.

Remember: The most important things in life are not things at all. (don't worry beloved, I have this saying on my wall because I need to see it daily too).

The first time you get your first paycheck, you may want to be prepared to call your mentor. I know I cried when seeing the amount of that check.

Anger: This one is huge. MOST girls experience anger. The spirit of anger has become our protector and our defender in the game. We need to learn how to let him go and partner with Jesus to be our defender and protector. Jesus wants desperately to help us, but he is a gentleman... He will never force himself on us. We must invite Him.

Men: Either seeking to only have a male boss or seeking NOT to have a male boss. Talking to men in the church about your problems, or playing that victim role with men in your life is an old behavior that is not of God. Seek wise counsel from women and ask the Holy Spirit to lead and guide you in whom you approach.

Another thing I have noticed is women who get saved tend to start feeling the need to date right away. It is like they never got to experience that part of their life and they find it exciting to be normal. That is great beloved, but only after you have dated Jesus and made Him your focus. Ask your mentor if you feel like you're ready to start dating and TRUST HER ANSWER!!

Authority: We all have had problems with authority in our life, or we wouldn't be here! We need to realize that there will always be an authority in our life. If it's not your parents and teachers, then it is your boss. If it is not your boss then it will be your future husband. If it is not your future husband, then it is your current husband: Jesus. HE is the head of the house. Pray for God to help you see the positive reasons we have authorities in our lives and to learn to accept, invite and admire them.

Here are a few reasons why I love authority: They keep us accountable to our actions, they keep us on the right track, they confirm the decisions we make, they will have to report to God for where they are leading. God will always bless my obedience to follow whom He places over me as my authority, regardless if they are wrong in where they are leading.

Impulsive: Oooooh sister- are we impulsive! This is a learned behavior and a sinful nature: two things against us. Thankfully, we have a mighty God! We have had to make quick decisions in the game to survive, stay safe or get the best trick. We are used to fast money and usually get what we need or want instantly. If we don't, we use our mouthpiece to get it. This sort of behavior is contradictory to Christ. Look at the fruit of the spirit listed above and circle the one that says: Patience.

Did you think God was kidding about patience in our life? Nothing worth having is going to come quickly.

One Sunday morning I was praying about my calling. I felt like it was taking years to get there and I was becoming discouraged and impatient. I cried out to God for help. He asked me the following questions, and I am going to do the same for you:

How long is a woman typically pregnant for?

_____

If the mother is very excited about her baby coming and just doesn't want to wait any longer, could she physically push the baby out at 4- 5 months?

_____

Even though it is impossible for a pregnant mother to push out her baby out at 4 or 5 months, what would happen to the baby if for some unexplainable reason, she could push it out early?

_____

_____

So… if she has waited the 9 months, and the baby has fully developed and her water breaks, can anyone stop a woman in labor?

---

When a woman has been implanted with a dream from God, it needs time to develop, but when it's ready, nothing will be able to stop it from coming forth. You can hold onto that promise!

Memories: Certain smells, songs or movies can trigger memories of events in our life. Sometimes we've stuffed those memories out because they were too traumatic, but eventually, they resurface. My husband was recently disciplining our toddler. She has been a dramatic, over-zealous little thing, pretending to cry to get her way. My husband said to her "stop faking it, get up and do what I asked you to do." Instantly I felt a rush of anger and heat pass through me. My thoughts went something like "how do you know if she is faking it, maybe she is upset. What kind of father are you that you don't believe your daughter. I can't believe I married someone so insensitive..." and on and on.

Normally, I would vocalize those thoughts out loud, and we'd end up in an argument which typically resulted in us not speaking for a day because my husband refuses to engage with me when my temper is at that level. THIS TIME, I went into my bedroom and allowed him to deal with our daughter. In my bedroom, I hit my knees, and I cried out to God, "Why do I feel like this? Why I am so angry at him?"

Right away, a memory I had forgotten about came to mind. My pimp was beating me, and I was covering my teeth so they wouldn't get broke (I have nice teeth). He punched me in the stomach, and it knocked the wind out of me, like had happened in school when I got a soccer ball in the gut. I was hunched over trying to breathe, crying and he violently grabbed me, "you're faking it. Get up before I beat you again."

I sat and cried in my bedroom over the memory. That one little, innocent, normal parenting incident could have gotten my husband and me into a fight, all because I didn't identify the trigger of a memory and recognize the anger and annoyance. I processed that memory with God that night rather than taking it out on my spouse, and I am so grateful I did.

Drama: Girl, sometimes we can become addicted to the drama. It can be exciting and intriguing; much more fun than the mundane routines of life. Rebuke that! God can make life exciting without drama. Ask Him, and He will provide. When you see drama surfacing in your life on a regular basis, it's time to hit your knees and ask God to break that habit that's developed. If you have more than one incident of drama a year, you may need to seek the Lord because life is not full of drama. It is full of meaningful relationships that will refine you and pour into your future!

Control: Our entire lives we have not been in control. Most of us come from some form of an abusive childhood; then we lashed out at teachers and friends. Now, we had our pimps over us telling us what to do, where to go and what to eat. It feels like a breath of fresh air when we finally have control over our own lives. But sometimes, we don't even realize that we can become quickly persuaded by the feeling of control, to control EVERYTHING around us.

Be cautious if you jump in during a conversation, you may be trying to control the conversation. Be cautious if you get worked up by your boss choosing the color of paint for your office. These, of course, are examples, but if someone was making a decision other than you, is causing you to partner with that old friend Anger - it's time to hit your knees beloved!

List behaviors that you feel you struggle with and/or the ones above that you can relate to:

_____

_____

_____

_____

_____

Anything can trigger these responses. You can tell you have a trigger, by recognizing when our thoughts partner with the opposite of the fruits of the spirit. Pray daily for the spirit of God to fill you and help you to be receptive to his guiding. God will never steer us wrong. Even in times when we can't see why He is not opening a door, we must TRUST that He is in control and He knows what is best for your future!

Garth Brooks says it best in one of his old country music songs, "Some of God's greatest gifts, are unanswered prayers."

This was a long chapter and you did great! I just really want to take some time to commend you for the amount of work and effort and energy you are putting into yourself. You are the temple of Christ and if you allow Him, he will do great things with your life. Good job sticking in there. This chapter is one that the enemy would love for you to forget, so please, go back through it a second time and/or journal about what really stood out to you. Feel free to write it in the space provided so it sticks in your mind. Bless you and know that I have been praying for you!

_____

_____

_____

_____

_____

# CHAPTER NINE

---

## Equipping Families of Victims

Why would I put a chapter in here for your family? Well, a couple of reasons:

I would love for you to share this chapter with whomever you are going to be living with.
I want you to see the benefits of being in a strong family structure.
I want to expose the lies about "family" that you may have been taught as a child.

What is "normal" and do you want it?

Most of us have been brought up in dysfunctional homes. Let's face it, what home ISN'T dysfunctional?? But, some of us, more than others.

You may not be even returning to your actual parents for this very reason. Some of you may be staying with a friend or family member until you can get your place. Some of you may be in a group home healing until you're ready to conquer the world on your own. Others possibly have been brought out of the life by a church member or other religious organization. Whatever your situation is. GOD HAS YOU RIGHT WHERE HE WANTS YOU!

So how do we walk out this new life? How do we become normal? Do we even want normal?

Let's expose the first lie:

1. What is Normal?

How you grew up as a child does NOT dictate how you have to live as an adult.

If your home did things that you wish it hadn't, then break the cycle now. Stand in the gap and start being that prayer warrior for your future home. Break the generational curses that surround your family. YOU DO NOT HAVE TO RUN YOUR HOME LIKE YOUR MOM DID; believe that!

In my life, my idea of "normal" consisted of dad drinking while mom would yell and scream and throw things. I'd hide under the bed during one of their nightly, volatile blow outs. When my first pimp hit me, I wasn't as shocked as maybe a healthy child would have been. I assumed this was how most adults fought behind closed doors.

When I made a vow to the Lord, I wanted to learn how to be a Godly wife while fighting. WOO HOO was that hard! Couples disagree, and I had to learn how to disagree in a godly manner: without throwing things, cussing and screaming - especially in front of my kids. I wanted to change my children's view of "normal" so they could have a good example to follow.

List some things that you would like to do differently in your home as a new Woman of God:

_____

_____

_____

_____

_____

Surround yourself with people that will help show you how to accomplish the list you just made.  Pray and ask God to bring Godly women in your life that will show you how to be a Christian Wife or Mother for your future.

There can be so many areas that may seem "normal" but have no place in the kingdom of God.  Handling these things, the way your family did may only lead you down a bitter path, or may trigger some of your old behaviors.

Here are a few that I have had to change in my own life, that I thought were normal:

Disagreeing/Fighting – (truth statement: There is a healthy righteous indignation that only comes from the Holy Spirit)
Finances – (truth statement: You can live off a normal budget)
Gossip – (truth statement: Why bother with spreading vicarious drama – focus on positivity.)
Murmuring and Complaining – (truth statement: Be thankful for what you have and trust that it's exactly what God wants you to have.)

Can you think of any more negative patterns or behaviors that you were taught growing up that you desperately want God to weed from your heart?  List them, then take the time to pray for each one with our prayer example we used in Chapter Two, by asking the Lord to replace with the opposite.

_____

_____

---

You want to read a good story about how the children of Israel murmured and complained concerning what they had, and how God felt about it.
Read Numbers 11:10-35

SISTER TIP: In case you are back in the home that you want desperately to be nothing like (I know this is true for a handful of you), use this an opportunity to hit your knees more frequently.  God allows situations in our life to draw us closer to Him.  Instead of partnering with anger or rage as your defender and protector, start learning how to partner with Jesus.  If you can get through this, beloved, there is NOTHING the devil can throw at you that you won't overcome!!!

2. New Surroundings

When you get back to your hometown, it can be easy to pick up where you left off.  Call up your old friends, let them know where you've been or what you're doing now.  It can be easy to go to the same hot spots you use to hang out at.

This is only because this is all you know.

Imagine your surrounds as a new adventure - SEEK OUT ways to have fun that is different than what you use to do.  SEEK OUT new people that are different than who you use to hang out with.

WIPE YOUR SLATE CLEAN - because God has.  This is your opportunity to start fresh.

Always wanted to try a new church?  NOW IS THE TIME!  See what programs they have for either single adults, or youth groups.  Maybe they even have an "ex-industry worker" group as I have seen in some churches. These are great ways to learn more about the word of God and to find other girls just like you that want to live a Godly life.

SISTER TIP: It can be very tempting to go back to old behaviors. This is not only a trap from Satan but your opportunity to show God your commitment. Do not take this step lightly!

"Therefore, if anyone is in Christ, he is a new creation; old things have passed away; behold, all things have become new." - 2 Corinthians 5:17 (NKJV)
You are a new creation - do butterflies leave the cocoon and go back to crawling on their bellies? No! They spread their wings and explore this new world in the sky; same world, just new surroundings.
List some new places in your area that you have never been and would like to try. Maybe your past made you feel stupid or unworthy to go to any of these. Don't let the enemy rob you of a great new experience!

_____
_____
_____
_____
_____

3. Why do we want to go back?

Believe me beloved- this does not mean just back to your old pimp. This can mean going back to old ways or old behaviors even. Calling up those ex-boyfriends, calling your old friends, or all of these above are a few common examples!

I am not judging here, shoot I went back to my pimp several different times. I'd run and try to get normal, but it was hard.

I slept on the couch with my daughter at my aunt's house and had to get on welfare for the first time. I was humbled and humiliated. I hadn't changed my number and "my man" was texting me how much he missed me and wanted me back. I hadn't made any Godly friends yet, and I didn't start getting involved in my church. I'd go on Sundays and pick at the pastor's sermon and find all the flaws. I was not breaking old habits. Yes, I was out from under my trafficker, but I was still acting like the old me.

It didn't take long for my trafficker to fly to my hometown to get me. And I went. I missed my home, my bed, my car. I missed getting anything at the grocery store that I wanted, and not having only to buy what was on sale or out of the coupon book. I missed having wife-in-laws to talk to and hang out with and go on "spa days" like our man let us sometimes do. Of course it didn't help that he reminded me of all that I missed and filled my cup with all the promises that he knew would sink a hook in me. Besides I was also afraid. Afraid he'd cause a scene, hurt me in front of my family or even worse hurt them. He was so unpredictable it just all seemed easier to comply and return.

It did not take much for my mind to invite Satan to play on the playground with me.

If you want a new life beloved, Christ is eager to give it!

Let's pretend you started dating someone. Roll with me on this, okay?

You guys are dating - he is taking you out to dinner on the weekends and calling or texting a little throughout the week. You just met, so you're still getting to know each other. No commitment yet.

Let's say he told you that he wanted to date other people. Those words might make you feel like he doesn't like you very much if he is unwilling to commit to you. However, you let it go and convince yourself that you are "just dating."

So, what happens if the next question he asks you, is to buy him a home and a car? Seems crazy, right? You still following me?????? This dude doesn't want to make me his exclusive girlfriend or marry me, he wants to date other people, but he still wants ME to provide for HIM?

THIS IS HOW GOD FEELS ABOUT US when we are indecisive of serving Him. I'm not talking about works resulting in love or blessing, don't miss the point here – I'm referring to being double minded and luke-warm in who you want to serve – good or evil.

Why would he want to provide all of these things to us if we cannot commit?

SISTER TIP: Make a decision now who you want to be: the caterpillar or the butterfly and then set your mind on the sky and never look back!

Do you feel the Holy Spirit prompting you to break some habits that you have started since coming home? Expose them now:

_____
_____
_____
_____
_____


4. The importance of New Habits:

I think numbers 1-3 made it pretty clear of why it is important to create new habits, and it gave us some great examples of how to do that.

I want to drive home this point though beloved:

You need to go after this new life with the same zeal and zealousness that you went after the old one.

If you were using drugs, and a plate of cocaine or meth got knocked off the table, you would be on your knees picking every bit up!  Not only did you want that high, but it was expensive.

GOD AND HIS WORD ARE EQUALLY AS VALUABLE AND MORE IMPORTANTLY SISTER, YOU ARE THAT VALUABLE!

If you freelanced for tricks, you did not let the word "NO" slow your night down or get you discouraged.  You would just keep approaching dudes until you got a date.

DONT LET CLOSED DOORS FROM GOD GET YOU DISCOURAGED: THIS IS HIS WAY TO GET YOU EXACTLY WHERE HE WANTS YOU.

If your trafficker wanted you to learn his ways quickly and gave you rules to obey and words to use, you listened out of fear, out of a desire to please him, out of a desire to belong to his family and impress.

THINK OF JESUS AS YOUR MAN NOW.  BUT A GOOD MAN, A MAN THAT ONLY HAS GREAT PLANS FOR YOU.  FOLLOW, LISTEN AND OBEY HIM WITH AS MUCH DESIRE!  HE DESERVES MORE RESPECT THAN ANYONE!

Can you think of some things you did with extreme zeal?
How can you turn those around to go after the things of
God?

_____

_____

_____

_____

_____


SISTER TIP:  Make an effort to get into your bible and pray
DAILY. this will be the only way for you to get to know His
voice and learn His ways.  Without it, we will perish for lack
of knowledge.

# CHAPTER TEN

---

## Are You Ready? Positioning Yourself for Revelation

Being in the "industry" of public speaking and mentoring for some time now, there seem to be some basic principles that gauge whether we, as survivors, still have some things to work on. Now that I am married, have children, am in ministry and have owned my businesses, there are new lessons and new issues that rise to the surface. Issues that would not have surfaced until I was in those situations: that's why they didn't show up until now.

So, what do you have to look forward to? Maybe if you are on the lookout for it now, it can save you an awful fight with your partner, a demotion in ministry or a heartbroken child. They say the smartest people learn from other's mistakes. I know you are smart dear sister, so I am praying you can learn from mine too. One thing I try to do on a continual basis is position myself for revelation. What does that mean? Always be on the lookout for what you can change in yourself. Never think that you have made it or are over things- God will ALWAYS take you deeper. You can never out do Him.

Any word you are given, book you read, song you hear or situation you are put in, is an opportunity to shift your mindset. Here are a few revelations God has given me years after my initial healing from sex trafficking:

## HIDE IT IN YOUR HEART

One morning, I was speaking at a church sharing my testimony and raising awareness on the local epidemic concerning human trafficking. My real father had never heard my full testimony. I didn't want to hurt him or make our family look bad and possibly embarrass them, so I had never invited him prior.

Uninvited and unannounced as I was getting ready to go onstage, my father walks in. He heard I was speaking and wanted to hear. I got nervous for the first time and started rethinking my testimony and how I could avoid certain points.

I went to my prayer director and asked for prayer. She gave me a great word that matured me right at that moment. That's the power of positioning yourself for revelation: never thinking you're finished, always looking for something to give you that "ah ha" moment.

Her words were: "You don't HAVE to tell us everything. There are some things that are ok to be private."

Sister Tip: When or if you say or think: "Oh, I know" or "Oh Ya, I've dealt with that" it is apparent to those around you that you don't have a teachable spirit and haven't matured in that area.

Let's look at the biblical principle that supports keeping things private. Turn with me if you will, to Luke 2:19. Now, what I'd like you to do, if you have an "ah ha" moment from this, is highlight it in your bible and write the date next to it. It is so much fun to look back years from now when God gives you this verse again and remember today.

I'll preface the Scripture by setting the stage for you. Mary had just given birth to Jesus, wrapped him in swaddling clothes and set him in a manger. The Wise Men came to visit with gifts and could tell that this was the scene fulfilling all the prophecies and promises that Jesus was, in fact, the Messiah. They told Mary and Joseph all the marvelous "things" that made them come to this revelation.

And Luke 2:19 (NKJV) reads:
"But Mary kept all these things and pondered them in her heart."

That word **kept** in Greek is syntre? And it means:

1)   to preserve (a thing from perishing or being lost)

Mary preserved all the things she was told and pondered them in her heart.

Now, the word PRESERVE in our English dictionary has the meaning:
1. to keep alive or in existence; make lasting: to preserve our liberties as free citizens.
2.   to keep safe from harm or injury; protect or spare.
3.   to keep up; maintain: to preserve historic monuments.
4.   to keep possession of; retain: to preserve one's composure.
5.   to prepare (food or any perishable substance) to resist decomposition or fermentation.

Have you ever been told something amazing about your future? Have you ever had something happen in your past? Those are the "things" that we're referring to in this instance.

The encouraging words given to Mary about her son being the Messiah, she "kept," she "preserved." God said it's ok to preserve those things. It is ok, to keep safe from harm or to protect. It's ok beloved, to maintain, to retain and to resist these things from allowing decomposition. It's ok TO NOT SHARE EVERY DETAIL.

"But Mary kept all these things and pondered them in her heart." The second part of that verse: "pondered them" is also amazing. Don't you just love nuggets from God?

The word *ponder* in Greek is *symball* and it means to bring together in one's mind or to confer with one's self.

Are you still following me beloved? Ok, last word and then we're going to throw them all together.

"Them"; She pondered THEM in her heart. What is "them?" Well, in Greek it is "en," and it means in, but when you put that together: "she pondered in in her heart," that just didn't make sense. So, I found that VERY same Greek word "en," used in another verse in Matthew 1:18 and it reads: "she became pregnant through the power of the Holy Spirit."

en = through

en = production of life from the Holy Spirit.

So, after translated from Greek, we can put it all together:

*The things that have happened to us and the promises that God has given to us, we DONT HAVE TO TELL EVERYONE EVERYTHING. We can preserve, we can keep alive, we can protect these things and confer with ourselves whether this will produce life, and especially life from the spirit. WILL IT EDIFY? WILL*

*IT GROW?  WILL IT MATURE THE THINGS OF
GOD IF I SHARE? Those are questions you should ask
yourself (or confer with self) before sharing either your
promise or your past: Will it produce life?*

That gives me chills, did you get them?

While the full development of that lesson came later in my
life, right when the prayer director was telling me it is ok
NOT to share, that verse about Mary hiding things in her
heart came into my memory.  I felt peace not sharing some of
my childhood with the audience that morning.

Now, don't forget: when the Lord blesses, the devil messes so
be on guard for a fight.  The enemy would love to come in
and snatch that revelation and tell a lie such as: "if you omit
it, it is a lie..."  But, what do we do when the enemy lies to us?
We capture that thought, and we counter it with a truth
statement, which is the word of God.  Tell the devil: "I can
hide things in my heart if it does not bring life, just like Mary
did."

Let's explore a promise that God gave you for your future.
Just like Mary, God had an amazing calling for her: to raise
the Messiah.  Could you imagine the pressure of being Jesus's
mom?  Do you spank Jesus as a toddler if he touches fire?
Do you put him in time out?  Did Jesus even have a "terrible
twos?"  What are the policies for raising the son of God?
What if you parent wrong, will He end up NOT the Messiah?
Will people be out to hurt or harm him if I tell people who he
is?

I can only imagine, since Mary was human, she had all these
fears and worries.

Because of that, God had her hide this promise in her heart
for quite some time.  Telling everyone the promises that God

gave you will not PRESERVE them. I am not saying not to tell anyone, but trust the Holy Spirit in you when you have that discernment that maybe it isn't time to share with this person. Negativity, worry, and fear can be like cancer to the Christian if we don't protect our promises. It will be just like scattering seeds along a path for the birds to come and eat.

3 "Then he told them many things in parables, saying: "A farmer went out to sow his seed. 4 As he was scattering the seed, some fell along the path, and the birds came and ate it up. 5 Some fell on rocky places, where it did not have much soil. It sprang up quickly because the soil was shallow. 6 But when the sun came up, the plants were scorched, and they withered because they had no root. 7 Other seed fell among thorns, which grew up and choked the plants. 8 Still, other seed fell on good soil, where it produced a crop—a hundred, sixty or thirty times what was sown. 9 Whoever has ears, let them hear." - Matthew 13:3-9 NIV

Do you have a promise from God that you haven't told anyone? I am not going to ask you to write it down, so don't worry! I am going to ask that you spend some time in prayer right now asking God to fan into flames that calling and promise for your life. Bring it to the forefront of your mind. If you feel you have not received one yet, then pray right now and ask God to give you one.

I'll wait beloved while you talk to the King.

***

WHO IS YOUR PROTECTOR?

I am not going to say that this next lesson is going to be easy. In fact, most people allow it to go right over their head. The usual response is, "Ya, sister Jesus is my protector..." However, their actions show different and quite frankly, that type of answer shows exactly where you are at still believing that you have settled ALL issues in your heart and grown to completion.  Even though the Bible says none of us will be perfect until the day we reach heaven, some still believe that they have it all together.

"Then Jesus said, "Whoever has ears to hear, let them hear." - Mark 4:9 (NIV)

These are mind changes, paradigm shifts, revelations, ah-ha moments that have come up in my walk.  It is not meant to hurt or offend.  I simply, want to give you a roadmap for the pitfalls ahead to avoid hurts.

About six years into my escape from human trafficking and my reconnection with the Lord, I was feeling restored and redeemed.  But, do you remember that onion diagram?  Well, dear sister it doesn't end.  I am not sure if it ever will.  I am pretty sure that God will be molding me and you until the day we die.

So, six years into my transformed life, I had a friend really hurt me.  I am not going to go into details because it won't bring life- but I am going to be transparent.  I hope you don't mind me talking about real issues, in real life, with real survivors and real women...

My friend allowed her children to treat mine very poorly and it became awkward and uncomfortable at church during Sunday school and at birthday parties and other gatherings. I felt like I was always on guard ensuring my kids weren't hurt while she never noticed.  And I felt angry and frustrated that she never noticed!  When trying to talk to her about it, or anything really, she got extremely offended and had lost many, many friends over her sensitive "offense" to anything anyone ever said or did. I prayed for months and truly felt that the Lord wanted me to write her a letter.

From friend to friend, in the letter, I not only confronted the way my children were treated but also how easily offended she got constantly. I told her that God wanted to give her a life of full, rich friendships and she was driving people away. I expected her, I guess, to see where she was going wrong and mature, continuing to be friends, with her paying a little closer attention to her children and responses.

WRONG! The letter blew up in my face, and she cried, stormed out of the middle of church, literally pushing past me to get out of nursery and was obviously completely offended (I don't know why I expected different). I thought: *"Oh well, right? I am from the streets, and I can cut ties real quick. Some friends you just have to love from a distance, Amen? SHE has issues."* I smiled, made a point not to gossip about it and moved on, feeling good that I did my part by obeying the Lord and writing the letter, even if it didn't get the response I had hoped for.

I moved on with that thought, patting myself on the back for how much I had grown in the way I responded. Even though my thoughts of cutting ties might not have been the healthiest, the old me would have socked the girl in the face and told her about herself! So, yes this was improvement. However, right when you have one area conquered, God wants to take you to the next level.

If things couldn't have gotten any worse, they did! Later that evening, her husband sent me a private email rebuking me for writing her a letter. SISTER... SISTER...SISTER... I went crazy. I will not lie.

I started yelling at my husband demanding that he call that man and rebuke him - and who does he think he is talking to me like that- and how dare he, he is not my leader nor my husband- and on and on until I fully partnered with rage!

152

Now, I am only this transparent because I cannot imagine I am the only survivor out there who has gone crazy before. I thought all of "that" was gone, but apparently, it had been hiding in my heart, waiting for something to brew that would be big enough to make it rear its ugly head.

I began manifesting thoughts of grabbing a bat and going to their house and beating them both up. Obviously, that is not of God. I could remember the last time I felt that angry as I sat there seething and cursed at them in my home. Six years prior I was cooking dinner and became so angry and full of rage, I wondered if my trafficker would taste poison if I put it in his food. From there, another memory flooded of me at around age ten, sitting in our pantry, trying to put my abusive mom's boyfriend's gun together. I imagined killing him, walking in the room, him hearing the squeak in the floor and waking up only to see me with a gun and kill me. So, I never did more than just spin the revolver around, trying to figure that hand gun out.

Now, I am not saying that any of that is right. I am only saying, that being abused for so long by my pimp and remembering watching my mom getting hurt, caused me to have murderous thoughts. That rage-ful, murderous spirit crept in at ten, and I had no clue it was still there. For six years even after my escape from trafficking, it continued to hide in my heart. God needed to bring it out and remove it!

Thankfully, instead of going to their home that night, I went to my friend and prayer warrior's house. She said she didn't even recognize me when I knocked at the door and she grabbed some holy oil and started praying over me. She said the most profound statement that radically changed my life:

"Men have overstepped their boundaries in your life, much like you feel this man did today. You have also felt like men have not come to your defense when they should have, much like your husband tonight.  You have been partnering with rage as your protector and defender for far too long, and it's time to let Jesus be that protector and defender."

Not only did that radically change my life right then and there as I rebuked that spirit and asked the Lord to fill its place with the Holy Spirit, but I knew I couldn't be the only one.

SISTER TIP: When you get angry or offended, stop and ask yourself what "feeling" comes to mind as your first response. I would care to guess that you have been partnering with that feeling as your protector.  I am not saying this is every time you get angry- but when you have a situation in your life that causes you to be EXTREMELY annoyed, frustrated, angry or hurt... there is a reason.

Now, I'm not talking about everyday annoyances, though those come up too.  I am talking about when we get extreme and out of control. Did the Lord allow that situation to show me what was still lingering in my heart? Is that why he prompted me to write her a letter? Could this have been nothing about teaching my friend about her offended spirit, but about pulling the weed of Murder from my heart?

Healthy hearts and minds do NOT act irrationally when someone hurts them.

Another thing during my time in ministry is I ask myself "How would Sister Linda respond?"  Sister Linda is my pastor's wife and one of the most amazing women of God I know.  When in doubt, and not seeming to get an immediate answer from the Lord, I ask myself how she would respond to that statement or person, and I try my best to do the same.

Do you have a person that you respect and admire that you can ask yourself, "How would they respond?"  Write their name here: _____

Do you have a time in which you find yourself EXTREME? What is the feeling that immediately hits you? Annoyance, Frustration, Anger, Depression, Close Off?

_____

Can you identify that spirit as something you have partnered with as your partner in crime in the past? If so, explain when:

_____
_____
_____

Are you ready to partner with Jesus instead?

_____

Let's pray:

Lord, I lift my sister up to you, and I pray God that she feels your presence right now. As I am typing this, you know each and every person whom this will touch. Invade her heart and mind Holy Spirit. Reveal to my sister the negative thoughts and actions that she has partnered with throughout her time as a child, into her exploitation and may still be following her into her newfound freedom. Lord, we bind that spirit of _____ and command it to leave. It is not welcome here in this child of God and has no place near the King. It no longer has any dominion over this body. We pray that your Holy Spirit would fill that partnership in her heart and her responses to situations. That she can whole heartedly walk with you in all things. Jesus, we want to partner with you as our protector and defender because we trust you. We trust that your plans for us are to prosper us and not to harm us. Thank you for revealing deeper issues in us that took years to surface. We love you, and we praise you.
In Jesus Name,
Amen.

Changing the Cloak of Bondage

How many of you have traded one bad habit for another?
Like maybe you stopped smoking, but now you NEED gum
all the time. You don't have a pimp anymore, but you feel a
desperation to have friends close at all times- maybe a co-
dependency that hasn't healed yet. This sort of mentality we
see in the game often, and that old behavior doesn't always go
away when we get saved. There is nothing new under the
sun, including the enemy's tactics.

It is easy to identify our negative thoughts and take them
captive. But what about when they are positive thoughts or
even Bible verses that Satan is using to distract you from
being on the right path? He can be just a click of the knob
off from the truth; lies are not always drastic.

Have you ever been jealous over some else's promotion or
blessing? _____

We all have! Take some time to list things you have been
jealous of. Seeing where your jealousy is most frequent is a
great starting place for prayer.

_____
_____
_____
_____


Awhile back, I went to a gathering event full of people
involved in the fight against human trafficking. It was
amazing, and I was truly honored to be there. This was a
conference full of men and women, saved and unsaved. As a
believer and full of the Holy Spirit, one evening God gave me
a revelation and paradigm shift.

I watched and chatted at a dinner while in the spirit I saw
jealousy and coveting slithering like snakes above everyone.

156

Now, because I am a believer, I knew that it wasn't the people, it was the spirits. "For we are not fighting against flesh-and-blood enemies, but against evil rulers and authorities of the unseen world, against mighty powers in this dark world." (Ephesians 6:12NLT). I went back to my hotel later that night and talked to the Lord. I had met lots of amazing survivors, whose fight was genuine, however, they were not believers. My heart was so troubled I began to cry, and I started talking to the Lord:

"Not everyone who escapes from Human Trafficking believes in you Lord? You didn't set them free? There are some people there who were set free by Satan?"

"Yes," The Lord replied, "He has switched their cloak of bondage. "No, they are not being beat and raped, but they are still slaves to self-promotion, fame and importance. Their handcuffs are just fuzzy now."

What an image! The only true road to freedom is the road leading to Jesus; otherwise, we are only slaves to something else. This may offend some of you. I pray it doesn't.

1 Therefore, laying aside all malice, all deceit, hypocrisy, envy, and all evil speaking, 2 as newborn babes, desire the pure milk of the word, that you may grow thereby,3 if indeed you have tasted that the Lord is gracious. 1 Peter 2:1-3
9 But you are a chosen generation, a royal priesthood, a holy nation, His special people, that you may proclaim the praises of Him who called you out of darkness into His marvelous light; 10 who once were not a people but are now the people of God, who had not obtained mercy but now have obtained mercy. 1 Peter 2:9-10

"**Chosen**" in Greek is eklektos
Defined as:
* picked out, chosen

* chosen by God,
* to obtain salvation through Christ
* Christians are called "chosen or elect" of God
* the Messiah is called "elect," as appointed by God to the most exalted office
  conceivable
* Choice, Select, the best of it's kind or class

That definition should give us all a different idea of what a "choosing fee" or "choose up" term in the game is. What a subtle yet impactful word, until you hear the true meaning of God himself!

Have you ever caught yourself having selfish motives? What about coveting someone else's blessing or open door? "I wish I was doing that... Why didn't I get to do that?"

Read the scripture found in Roman 12:15
"Rejoice with those who are rejoicing. Cry with those who are crying."

_____

I think it would be helpful to write this scripture out and let it really sink in and take root in your heart. I left a line beneath the verse just for you!

Next, list the motives for which you are doing the things you are doing. Whether you're sharing your story publicly, getting married, working in ministry or whatever else God may have called you into, make a list of the reasons why you are doing it.

_____

_____

_____

_____

Remembering these things can be helpful when a slithering spirit of jealousy tries to invade your heart. Remind that spirit that you don't fight against flesh and blood, that we are called to rejoice with others that are rejoicing, and through that selflessness, God will bless you!

Relationships

This is something that survivors ask me about a lot. What it's like being married with children? Do triggers come up? How did you know he was the one? How long were you saved before you got married, etc.?

There is no specific answer to knowing when you're ready to date or when you're ready to get married. God, however, does have a specific plan and learning to trust Him and learning to hear His voice will give you a much better direction when you are ready.

This is such a vast topic; it could be an entire book all in itself. However, there are three points that I felt the Lord wanted my touch on.

1.   God brought Adam his partner Eve AFTER he stepped into his calling:

19 So the Lord God formed from the ground all the wild animals and all the birds of the sky. He brought them to the man to see what he would call them, and the man chose a name for each one. 20 He gave names to all the livestock, all the birds of the sky, and all the wild animals. But still, there was no helper just right for him.
21 So the Lord God caused the man to fall into a deep sleep. While the man slept, the Lord God took out one of the man's ribs[d] and closed up the opening. 22 Then the Lord God made a woman from the rib, and he brought her to the man.- Genesis 2:19-22
Sometimes, we need to stop focusing on a partner and on finding a husband and start focusing on what God is calling us to do. Like Adam, God called him to start naming the

animals. As he was doing this, God brought him Eve. Not before, not after. Remember that beloved.

2.   There is NO "perfect" marriage.

This is such a crucial point to set in really. Let's write it down big and bold:

After my husband and I got married, we had some issues, yes. I got upset by certain words or didn't like the way he parented the children, etc. I started feeling like "I" had issues because of my past. I started believing the lie that if I got healing from my past that our marriage would be better. I started self-hating and blamed my past for my marriage.

While of course emptying my baggage made the load lighter, the truth is NO ONE HAS A PERFECT MARRIAGE.

Couples without trauma like ours still have issues- all marriages have times when the partners disagree when one does something that offends the other. This is marriage. Do not for one-second beloved think it's you, your past or your problems. This is normal marriage. With the Holy Spirit, you guys together can learn to work things out in a healthy way.

I encourage you to attend a marriage class that talks about generational curses and soul ties. These two topics will free both of you from issues of your past. If your church does not offer a marriage class that teaches those two things, find some books that you both can read together.

- Breaking Generational Curses
- Breaking Soul Ties

3.   Together you are called to be ONE:

"9 Two people are better off than one, for they can help each other succeed. 10 If one person falls, the other can reach out and help. But someone who falls alone is in real trouble. 11 Likewise, two people lying close together can keep each other warm. But how can one be warm alone? 12 A person standing alone can be attacked and defeated, but two can stand back-to-back and conquer. Three are even better, for a triple-braided cord is not easily broken." Ecclesiastes 4:9-12 NLT

My husband and I were both nearing thirty when we got married. We had been single, independent adults for a long time before God brought us together. I was a single mother and had already traveled the world speaking out against forced prostitution. How do you mold two independent lives?

At first, my husband seemed too laid back. I was unsure if his slow-moving pace would match with my fast-moving ways. While engaged, I began to doubt that I heard the Lord correctly. I got on my knees one night in prayer- I turned on worship music, and I refused to leave that position until I heard from the Lord. The next thought that came from God moved me:

"The most effective boats have both a motor and an anchor. Two anchors would make a boat sit stagnate, and two motors would send you spiraling in crazy directions."

God showed me that my husband and I TOGETHER would be a great team and effective in what God was calling US to. Instead of seeing it as a "mine and his" thing, I started seeing it as a "we." I countered any doubt with the following truth statements:

- You will not reach your calling without him

- Use each other's gifts to your advantage

Yes, "using" can be a word that brings some negative connotation with it. However, it was the only thing that made my mind click. Instead of focusing on what he did differently than me and complaining in my mind about his lack of administrative qualities, for example, I started seeing us two members of a team that needed each other in order for the team to win.

If we both were great at book keeping, but neither of us good at going out and marketing, then we wouldn't be very effective at running our business or getting bills paid. If our team had two great quarter backs but no one good at catching the throw, what good what it be? The quarterback should not be annoyed that the catcher can't throw- he should be grateful! Neither should the catcher be annoyed that the quarterback can't catch. Make sense?

Are you married or dating anyone? Are there some habits that bother you? Can you take some time to focus on the positive differences that he brings to the team? Maybe list them below:

_____

_____

_____

_____

_____

I listed several books as suggested reading in the back of this book. These books were very helpful in helping me learn about successful, God fearing relationships. Take some time to invest in your parenting skills and your marriage. Let's face it the way we use to be only got us to where we are now, so let's make new habits: today!

# CLOSING
# YOU DID IT!

Well my friend, this is it. YOU DID IT!!!! I am so proud of you! We covered a lot of material in regard to what girls like us experience.

This is life long journey. We do not get saved and get amnesia. Right when we think we finally have an area in our life under control, God reveals a little more sin that is still hidden in our hearts. The first time your pastor or spiritual authority rebukes you, it can bring up lots of feelings that you thought were gone. I encourage you to seek your mentor and Jesus with each trigger that comes up in your life. They will get easier to identify and manage, but they don't end. Sometimes, years go by until I get one, but when it comes it can be like a freight train!

I want to leave you with a bible study I heard at an ex-industry worker group. It made such an impact on me; I wanted to re-teach it to you. You are welcome to take your word out and follow along or highlight, or you can follow along with me below.

Luke 15:1-
New Living Translation (NLT)
Parable of the Lost Sheep
1 Tax collectors and other notorious sinners often came to
listen to Jesus teach. This made the Pharisees and teachers of
religious law complain that he was associating with such
sinful people—even eating with them!
So Jesus told them this story: "If a man has a hundred sheep
and one of them gets lost, what will he do? Won't he leave
the ninety-nine others in the wilderness and go to search for
the one that is lost until he finds it? And when he has found
it, he will joyfully carry it home on his shoulders. When he
arrives, he will call together his friends and neighbors, saying,
'Rejoice with me because I have found my lost sheep.' In the
same way, there is more joy in heaven over one lost sinner
who repents and returns to God than over ninety-nine others
who are righteous and haven't strayed away!

Parable of the Lost Coin
8 "Or suppose a woman has ten silver coins[a] and loses one.
Won't she light a lamp and sweep the entire house and search
carefully until she finds it? And when she finds it, she will call
in her friends and neighbors and say, 'Rejoice with me
because I have found my lost coin.' In the same way, there is
joy in the presence of God's angels when even one sinner
repents."

Parable of the Lost Son
11 To illustrate the point further, Jesus told them this story:
"A man had two sons. The younger son told his father, 'I
want my share of your estate now before you die.' So his
father agreed to divide his wealth between his sons.
13 "A few days later this younger son packed all his
belongings and moved to a distant land, and there he wasted
all his money in wild living. About the time his money ran
out, a great famine swept over the land, and he began to
starve. He persuaded a local farmer to hire him, and the man

sent him into his fields to feed the pigs. The young man became so hungry that even the pods he was feeding the pigs looked good to him. But no one gave him anything.

17 "When he finally came to his senses, he said to himself, 'At home, even the hired servants have food enough to spare, and here I am dying of hunger! I will go home to my father and say, "Father, I have sinned against both heaven and you, and I am no longer worthy of being called your son. Please take me on as a hired servant."'"

20 "So he returned home to his father. And while he was still a long way off, his father saw him coming. Filled with love and compassion, he ran to his son, embraced him, and kissed him. His son said to him, 'Father, I have sinned against both heaven and you, and I am no longer worthy of being called your son."

22 "But his father said to the servants, 'Quick! Bring the finest robe in the house and put it on him. Get a ring for his finger and sandals on his feet. And kill the calf we have been fattening. We must celebrate with a feast, for this son of mine was dead and has now returned to life. He was lost, but now he is found.' So the party began.

25 "Meanwhile, the older son was in the fields working. When he returned home, he heard music and dancing in the house, and he asked one of the servants what was going on. 'Your brother is back,' he was told, 'and your father has killed the fattened calf. We are celebrating because of his safe return.'

28 "The older brother was angry and wouldn't go in. His father came out and begged him, but he replied, 'All these years I've slaved for you and never once refused to do a single thing you told me to. And in all that time you never gave me even one young goat for a feast with my friends. When this son of yours comes back after squandering your money on prostitutes, you celebrate by killing the fattened calf!'

31 "His father said to him, 'Look, dear son, you have always stayed by me, and everything I have is yours. We had to

celebrate this happy day. For your brother was dead and has come back to life! He was lost, but now he is found!'"
You can see from this chapter in Luke that three examples were given:
The Lost Sheep
The Lost Coin
The Lost Son
God uses various analogies throughout the Bible and especially in this chapter. This is because not all of us identify with the same analogy. If I wanted to give an example to a painter, I wouldn't use terms related to baseball. However, if I wanted to share something with an athlete, it would benefit me to have my pocket full of analogies that are sports related. We learn this example from the master of analogies: God. So, let's break them down:
The Lost Sheep: We could imagine a sheep being lost and what might happen. He'd be alone out in the woods somewhere. He's probably crying looking around for the herd but nothing familiar in sight.
The shepherd left his entire flock to go find this one. THE SHEEP KNEW IT WAS LOST AND THE OWNER DESPERATELY WANTED IT HOME.
The Lost Coin: Unlike the sheep, the coin obviously had no thoughts or feelings. The owner of the coin, however, did and we can imagine the diligence she used when looking for it. She probably moved furniture, swept under rugs, and retraced her steps. THE COIN DIDN'T KNOW IT WAS LOST, BUT THE OWNER KNEW HOW VALUABLE IT WAS.
The Lost Son: This son was not lost, he knew he was far from home but didn't care. He rather has the pleasures of the world and goes through hard knocks then live in His father's home under His rules more than likely. Once he finally understood that even being a servant in his home was far better than eating with the pigs, he came home. HIS FATHER HELD NO JUDGEMENT AND ACCEPTED

HIS SON BACK TO HIS RIGHTFUL PLACE AS AN HEIR.

I ask you as we close this workbook together, which one are you?  Did you know you were lost like the sheep?  Were you oblivious to where you ended up but God knew your value like the coin?  Or were you like the son and blatantly left thinking more was out there and ended up with the pigs?

_____

_____

_____

_____


Either way, you're found now!!  God, your loving father, wanted you home and found and here you are!!  Embark on this new journey with excitement and gratefulness…  YOU WERE BORN FOR GREATNESS!!!

Dear Lord,

I lift my sister up to you today.  She is sitting before you, just finishing this book, which you God, put on my heart to share with her.  You have a great plan for her life, and I just pray that the words she has learned throughout this do not fall among the thorns for the birds to pick up, but they take root in the soil of her heart. May she live a vibrant, fulfilled life for you heavenly father.  Let not the enemy come in to steal her dreams, kill her hope or destroy her future.  I pray for a hedge of protection around her heart and mind as she decides to set her path toward you. Ordain her steps- go before her and make every crooked place straight.  Open doors that no man can open and shut doors that no man can shut. Surround her with Godly, wise counsel that will direct her in your ways oh Lord.  We love you, and we praise your might works!  Fill her with your Holy Spirit from the crown of her head to the soles of her feet.

In Jesus Name,

Amen

**Suggested Reading**

Books that have made a huge impact on my own personal success:

*         God's Leading Lady – TD Jakes

*         Dream Thieves – Rick Renner

*         Battlefield of the Mind – Joyce Meyer

*         Purpose Driven Life – Rick Warren

*         Five Love Languages – Gary Chapman

*         Becoming a Contagious Christian – Bill Hybel

*         What's in the Bible: A One-Volume Guidebook to God's Word – Robert Wolgemth and RC Sproul

*         Power of a Praying Wife - Stormy O'martian

*

> **Chapter Two: 40 Reasons She Won't Leave, taken from Women's Crisis in Grants Pass, Oregon and adapted by Rebecca Bender to fit sex trafficking survivors.**
>
> **Chapter Four: Journal Exercise taken from** The PTSD Workbook: Simple, Effective Techniques for Overcoming Traumatic Stress Symptoms **by** Mary Beth Williams **and Soili Poijula (May 15, 2002)**
>
> **Part II Introduction: Consulting concerning Neurophysiology provided by Nancy Trifilo, Held Captive No More.**

Made in the USA
Monee, IL
05 May 2021